A Vulnerable Teacher

# A Vulnerable Teacher

## Ken Macrorie
*Western Michigan University*

HAYDEN BOOK COMPANY, INC.
Rochelle Park, New Jersey

The following copyrighted material has been reprinted with permission:

Excerpts from Irving Babbitt's *Rousseau and Romanticism,* published by the Houghton Mifflin Company.

Anatole Broyard's review of *Death As a Fact of Life,* copyright © 1973, by The New York Times Company.

Excerpt from Ring Lardner's "Gullible's Travels," published by Charles Scribner's Sons.

Excerpts from E.M.W. Tillyard's *The Elizabethan World Picture,* copyright © 1944, by Macmillan Publishing Co., Inc.

Excerpts from L. Wiener's translation of *Tolstoy on Education,* copyright © 1967, by The University of Chicago Press.

*Library of Congress Cataloging in Publication Data*

Macrorie, Ken, 1918-
  A vulnerable teacher.

    1. Macrorie, Ken, 1918-   2. College teaching.
I. Title.
LA2317.M224A29 1974     378.1'2'0924     74-4070
ISBN 0-8104-5937-X
ISBN 0-8104-5936-1 (pbk)

1  2  3  4  5  6  7  8  9   PRINTING

74 75 76 77 78 79 80 81 82   YEAR

# Preface

The "vulnerable teacher" in the title of this book is me, and I am proud to call myself one. The vulnerability referred to is a strength, although it proceeds from what most persons would call weakness—a willingness to admit ignorance or inexperience while basing one's thought and action on his own experience.

After seventeen years of teaching I stumbled upon a way to enable students to perform acts that impressed them, their fellows, me, and persons outside the classroom. What they were doing was behaving vulnerably, bringing their experience up against the experience of the course, so that the two conversed, illuminated each other. When my students and I are learning most powerfully, we are ever remembering where we came from. And so there is some living going on in our learning place.

I have found that hundreds of other teachers in the country have stumbled onto the same discoveries. Some of them have asked me to record my experience without making it look easier than it is. I have tried to do that here.

K.M.

# Acknowledgments

Thanks to the people who helped me write this book. At the time they were John Bennett, high-school teacher; William E. Coles, Jr., English professor; Cynthia Costanza, free school director; Harriet Dye Wikum, English instructor; Bob Koehler, housepainter; Joyce T. Macrorie, jeweler and writer; Nancy Williams, high-school student. Special thanks to S. William Cook, Jr., and Robert Boynton, editors, who helped me believe that there are yet alive publishers who think of their books as something more than economic goods. And my appreciation to Western Michigan University for granting me a sabbatical leave in which to write this book.

# Contents

Lines printed in italics in this book were written by my students or the students of other teachers using the same approach. Throughout the book, whether indicated in the text or not, names have been changed wherever I think injury might occur to persons.

K.M.

## Chapter 1

# *Becoming Vulnerable*

☐

There is a time in every man's education when he arrives at the conviction that envy is ignorance; that imitation is suicide; that he must take himself for better, for worse, as his portion. . . . The power which resides in him is new in nature, and none but he knows what that is which he can do nor does he know until he has tried.

"Self-Reliance," Ralph Waldo Emerson

☐

When I went off to college I was scared. I lived in the isolationist Mississippi River valley in Moline, Illinois, 180 miles from Chicago, which breathed no influence on this clean town of 20,000 people except the conserved air trapped between the pages of Colonel McCormick's *Chicago Tribune*. My father, who loved to recite Shakespeare, had died six years earlier. My mother, a librarian, was planning to send me money every month to keep me at Oberlin College far off in Ohio—if I held on to the two-year scholarship I had been granted because I had the second-highest grades of any boy in my high school and had been editor of the school yearbook.

Neither Mother nor Father had gone to college, but my great grandfather had graduated from Middlebury long ago somewhere in the East and later had become superintendent of the public schools in a relatively cultured town across the river.

When I arrived in the town of Oberlin, population 2,000, plus 1,200 undergraduates, and about 800 more students divided between the Conservatory of Music and the Theological Seminary, I was head down with fear. Had never seen anything like that place before. A great grassy square in the center of town with towering elms, bricked walkways creating a huge X, and only one building—a memorial arch, something connected to the Boxer Rebellion as I remember. And a lot of money had been given to the college by the Kung family, which included the woman who became Madame Chiang Kai-shek. The arch and the Kung family seemed right. Everything was foreign to me.

The town didn't center around a farm-implement company as Moline did. Bordering the square were college buildings of all kinds, and on one side a block of commercial buildings which seemed also to belong to the college: the chain ice-cream store where the kids got cheap and indifferent sundaes; the corner drugstore where I was later to drink milk shakes in long, cool, stainless-steel vases; the bookstore where we had to go for all books and supplies; a photography studio which did the work for the college yearbook; a clothing store featuring college fashions.

In those days I was also scared of girls, having dated little in high school although burning with as much desire as I believe any boy ever experienced. Then I didn't sense it—I moved through the streets and buildings of Oberlin largely unperceiving, stunned by foreignness—but I suppose one disturbing fact was that girls were walking around everywhere without their mothers and fathers.

The men's dormitory was no more reassuring. There, right down the hall from my room (where I lived with an American missionary's son from Kyoto, Japan) resided a boy my age named Furwall, who seemed at least forty-two years old to me. The first night he arrived he made a date with the best-looking girl I had ever seen. And within a week he was telling us what it was like to explore her physically.

Classes were worse. I had thought I would be saved from social threats by books and teachers, being an "A" student back in Moline. Now I faced not teachers, but professors. One wore a Phi Beta Kappa key looped across his vest—as I was told by one of my Eastern acquaintances who recognized the hay in my clothes and demeanor. The professor was an expert in Dante and Milton, two men awesome to me because I had never read them.

Most of the time the professors threw me. They said things like "as it were" and "one can say." I didn't know for several weeks why that *it* got connected with a plural verb or who the *one* was that was mentioned by so many men at the front of the room.

Mr. Williams taught an introductory literature course and was so lively that I feared him less than the others. Once when he was lecturing on *Henry IV, Part I,* he took the roles of Prince Hal and Poins and the waiter Francis in the tavern and cavorted in front of us as he read the "Anon" lines which show Francis a dolt. Suddenly Professor Williams stopped and said, "You're supposed to be laughing. With freshmen I always have to say ahead of time, 'This is going to be funny' or they don't get the Elizabethan humor. So here I go again, and this is going to be funny." I laughed with all the other students, forced, hearty; but I didn't understand what was funny.

That year my grades averaged C+. I was supposed to maintain a B average to keep my scholarship. I got a letter saying I was on probation. At the end of my third semester I was called in to talk to the Director of Scholarships. I knew my mother had been skimping to supply me money for room, board, supplies, and a few treats. I thought this was the end; I prepared myself for a final trip to Moline, the boy who had let down his mother and failed his family's first opportunity in generations to go to college. But the Director said I could keep the scholarship. I should try harder.

I wanted to try harder. I wanted so badly that I crammed for the final exam period in the library of the Theological Seminary, which I had found out was the quietest place on campus. I read over my copious notes for a half hour, then dozed, my head on the table for ten minutes. That is where I taught myself to quick nap. I always woke up guilty.

I learned also to hitchhike to Cleveland, thirty miles away, with a friend who had played sax in a jazz band before coming to college. He and I spent many weekends listening to Duke Ellington and Glen Gray. There was dusky long-limbed Ivie Anderson sitting on the piano, then jitterbugging on it while she sang. I was thrilled, shaking. While I stood there on the dance floor in front of the band I didn't feel guilty. Furwall wasn't my companion, a lot of people stood around the band, no girls threatened me. It was foreign but it discovered for me an exotic region in my heart I hadn't known existed.

When I got back from each trip to Cleveland and faced a French class I wasn't prepared for, I felt guilty again.

In that second year I took a complete course in Shakespeare. We read every play he wrote and sat at the feet of a professor—Oberlin lecterns stood on platforms, some of them two feet high—who lectured three times a week in a soft, rapid-fire, cultivated voice on the play I had just not finished reading. The plays went by me in a rush. Olivia, Jaques, Desdemona, Gertrude, Bottom, Cassius—the names new to me remained new and were often forgotten before the weekly quiz. There may have been a question or two asked in that room by students but generally it was a one-voice hour. I was puzzled not to have become engaged with the plays. My father had liked Shakespeare, and he hadn't gone to college.

☐

After three years of fright and one in which I began to find powers in myself, I graduated from Oberlin, studied printing at Carnegie Tech —living by myself—returned to Moline and took on a job in the advertising department of the farm-implement company my father had worked in, and then volunteered to fight Hitler.

During my three years in the Army I had time to decide I wanted to go back to college and become an English professor. So I did that. For the subsequent twenty-five years I have been paid by the citizens of North Carolina, New York, California, and Michigan to do something called "teach" their children in universities. For the first seventeen years, many of the days went like this:

The students were sitting out there in straight rows looking over the backs of other students in the row in front—at me. Often I began my sentences with "Of course—" because I had been over the material many times and read it in the books and articles of authorities.

The students were not responding to my statements. I saw a fellow furtively spreading the school paper on the writing arm of his chair. A girl near the window was gazing out toward the sun. Most of the students were not thinking about what I was saying. Or questioning it. They were writing it down in their notebooks. Not all of it, but the high points—as I and dozens before me had ordered them to do. That means they were generalizing and abstracting what I said, although that had usually already been generalized and abstracted.

The best students (meaning those who got the highest grades) were putting down those of my statements likely to appear in the next quiz or the final exam. They would have been idiots to have spent their time writing down what interested them most. It was what interested me most that they concentrated on. Of course.

Up there at the lectern—or if I was affecting nonchalance and sitting on a table, my loud socks displaying an inch of skin above them—I was talking on my own. Every minute was mine, and the silences frightened me when I departed from notes and for a few seconds couldn't remember what I wanted to say next. The students knew that what I said was all mine, not theirs; and the chances were high that it would always be mine, for they would be giving it back to me soon on answer sheets and forgetting it the next morning. All mine, but "very important," as I said again and again during the lecture.

(I am looking back now and describing my teaching with insight I didn't possess in those days.)

From the lectern I kept insisting that it was all important, because the students did not seem aware that any of it was important. Many apparently did not think the course important. (Another of-course course whose materials belonged completely to me. What might actually be important in it for them was beyond their conjecture.) They had not been invited to bring any of their experience to bear upon the experience I was generalizing about. There were no handles for them. Finally, all they could guess is what might be important for me as I made up the test.

As I lectured, sometimes they could see I was warming up, getting in a stew or ecstasy about something, and they could guess that the idea counted for me. But it probably would not count for me in the test because I would be scholarly, objective. In making up the questions I would be careful not to ask something I felt strongly about, for later in grading I might show prejudice. So they saw—or thought they saw— that even my commitments were weak; and they were influenced not to reveal their commitments, and finally not to commit themselves at all in matters intellectual, social, or artistic, or whatever the bent of the course.

"Of course" was a fit phrase for me to strew through my lectures. It said there would be no surprise in what followed. It established my superiority. I generalized, abstracted, and then explained. I did not give the listeners two facts and challenge them to make something of them. Instead I quickly categorized the two and from that moment on those facts resided in drawers that I would pull out when I felt the need to. The listeners were not expected to go poking around in drawers when the impulse moved them, or to open an unlabeled drawer, or to stuff an empty one with any of their possessions.

As the years went by, I lectured less and less and conducted "discussions" more and more. I dominated the discussions. They became question and answer sessions in which I asked a question and then answered it myself with a little lecture.

□

For seventeen years I heard my students repeating badly to me what I had said to them and hundreds before them. I read their tired, hurriedly written papers conveying in academic dialect what they thought proper to give Teacher. One day in May in an Advanced Writing class I finally exploded. "I can't stand to read this junk any longer. Go back and write down as fast as you can whatever is in your mind—for fifteen minutes. Write so fast you can't think of punctuation or spelling or how you're going to say it. I would like for a change to read some truth that counts for you."

Since that day in 1964 I have turned my teaching around. Now in every course I begin by asking students to write anything that comes to their mind. Freed of the limitations and prohibitions common to academic writing assignments, they find unsuspected powers.

I then ask them to turn these powers upon the work of the course.

In Shakespeare class, for example, I ask students to read *Romeo and Juliet* and put down their reactions in journals.

> *There is nothing remote or unreal about Capulet, since to me he is much like my father. Capulet isn't always aware of what Juliet's up to. One minute he's paying some attention to her, and at other times he's not really thinking of her even though he may be talking about her. He is there for the big things—like marrying her off. It was always frustrating to me to have my dad on vacation because for two solid weeks he'd want to know everything I was doing, with whom, and all about this "whom." Juliet's father must have frustrated her too by only occasionally sticking his nose into her business. If a father is going to be that way, he at least ought to be consistent.*
>
> *It struck me funny to think of Capulet staying up half the night before the planned wedding between Paris and Juliet. He felt he was needed there to get the feast off to a good start. My dad, like Capulet, sometimes has funny, inconsistent notions. I remember him undertaking pickling his own pickles. Undertaking is right—he blew it and we buried them in the yard the next day.*

To a person unfamiliar with *Romeo and Juliet* that comment may seem trivial. Rather it is a shrewd portrait of Capulet, one of those minor characters whose human inconsistency Shakespeare established in short space. When I first read the play as I prepared to "teach" it, I found Capulet wanting as a dramatic character. Only as my students and I probed his actions by considering fathers of fourteen-year-old girls did I come to appreciate his complexity. Like other powerful Shakespeare plays, *Romeo and Juliet* slides by too fast on stage or film for a watcher to taste all its richness and character. That is why we *read* these plays more often than those of other playwrights.

Such readings by my students transformed my classes and my life. I became eager to go to classes; every one of them surprised me. I was not hearing my words and thoughts coming back to me. No longer did the papers begin:

> As far as the plot is concerned, King Lear *is very interesting because in reality there are two plots running along side by side or parallel. . . .*

No longer did the papers take up a number of topics and treat them with ridiculous brevity and superficiality:

> *Now I wish to turn from the subject of plot to the subject of characters. The characters in this play by the renowned dramatist are most interesting. They represent a wide range of character, from a young boy or fool to an old man who is losing his mind. Shakespeare has the great ability of showing you a wide diversity of tragic figures from all walks of life. Women as well as men walk through the pages of this play. . . .*
>
> *The poetry, or diction, of* King Lear *is also exceptional. It, too, is marked by a complexity and richness that is amazing. The wonder of Shakespearian tragedy is ever a mystery, a vague, yet powerful, tangible presence; an interlocking of the mind with a profound meaning, thus resulting in a greater significance for the reader. The richness of this most famous of all English writers in the level focus of creation that builds a massive oneness of single quality from a multiplicity of differentiated units. . . .*

Glub, glub, glub, as Jonathan Swift would say. All the sentences are pompous, including those which the student obviously stole from some critic. I am not certain which words above belong to the student, but I suspect that the passage beginning "The wonder of . . ." is all borrowed, except for the words "thus resulting in a greater significance for the reader." Probably the phrase "in the level" contains a typographical error and should read "is the level," but I don't really much care, for the whole passage reads like mush to me anyway. What critic was pilfered I do not know, and I am not going to begin reading all Shakespeare criticism in order to find out.

Since my students have begun to use their own voices in writing, I am more charitable toward those who in the past did not. Unconsciously I had pressed them to steal and pontificate and write emptily. They wrote with one purpose: to give me what they thought I wanted. I shudder at their conception of me. In those days my course did not engage students with the life in Shakespeare's plays. They felt little connection between it and their own lives, so they had no true base for writing their papers.

One day three weeks into a Shakespeare course one of my students who had suffered an eye injury and been absent after the first day turned in a paper which began:

> *Socialization and coexistence with fellow human beings is a delicate phenomenon or process which inherently follows the individ-*

*ual through his life. Obviously Shylock's attitude reflects a matur-
ation process laden with dislike and rejection of other-than-Jewish
people, and beyond this development to manhood, his present life
is also filled with reasons to dislike and injure, when possible, the
people who oppress him. . . .*

A girl in another class had dubbed this kind of language "Engfish." My
Shakespeare student had written a graduate-school strain of it.

☐

By January 1970, I had taught ten classes in Shakespeare which
delighted me and the majority of students. There was life in the classroom. I asked for honesty and got it.

*In Richard II, Mowbray swears to keep his nose clean while in
exile and doesn't complain enough about the unfairness of it. Of
course that may be unfair to Mowbray as I admit to having let
my mother or father order me about concerning dress, conduct,
and attitude, and I'm married, for God's sake, not even under
their jurisdiction any more. So maybe he isn't such a nut, merely
expedient. Upon reflection, it doesn't sound sensible to contem-
plate telling a king to go to hell.*

Commonly, naturally, students brought their own experience up against
the experience in Shakespeare's plays.

*After Bolingbroke has been banished from England, his father
says he should think of the banishment as traveling for pleasure.
His son replies:*

> *My heart will sigh when I miscall it so,
> Which finds it an enforcèd pilgrimage.*

*Last summer a good friend of my husband's was inducted into the
army. He had not yet graduated and his wife had only two more
courses to take. He was born here in Michigan and had many
friends and his family near him. He decided to go to Canada and
was very unhappy about it, not because he did not want to live
there, but because he was being forced to go (it was go to Canada
or go to jail). He and Bolingbroke both had the human need to
choose for themselves where to live.*

When I stopped giving tests because they did little more than
encourage students to say what they supposed I wanted them to say, a
few couldn't break their school habits. For example, here's a student
opening his paper:

*In Shakespeare's* Romeo and Juliet *my favorite character is Friar Lawrence because he's respected as an intelligent man, and he impresses me as being "cool," in control of his emotions, and always willing to help the young lovers out of trouble. His calmness and confidence dominate the chaotic action of the play. . . .*

The writer of that paragraph was plugged in to the old circuit. He thought his professor would like to hear that a friar was respectable: that's the way teachers are. It was probably a moot point to him whether or not Shakespeare thought of friars this simplistically; but it was the professor he had to please, not Shakespeare. So do the vinegar truths of the best writers become mollified.

After a few weeks in that class no student referred to a play as "Shakespeare's." They all recognized that they were not writing for Teacher but for all the human beings in the room, and however formal Teacher might be, no student wanted to be told that the play in question in a Shakespeare class was by Shakespeare.

Most of the students responded to the invitation to speak truths; for example,

*"I am the greatest, able to do the least." This statement by the Friar following the deaths of Romeo and Juliet in the tomb was made by a man and a humble one at that, but the nicest thing I can say about him is that he tried harder.*

*If he wasn't called Friar and if he didn't perform the marriage ceremony, I wouldn't have known him for anything other than a friend willing to help out in a pinch. I think it was too bad he didn't become humble before he started playing with other people's lives.*

*The Friar is Romeo's friend and counselor as well as his religious confessor. When Romeo approaches him about Juliet, he teases him about his previous passion for Rosaline and his sudden change of heart. "Thy old groans ring yet in mine ancient ears." (83:74) It surprises my logical self then that he agrees to marry them with no consideration of the possible consequences, his only reason being "For this alliance may so happy prove to turn your households' rancor to pure love." (84: 91-92)*

*I contend that if the Friar agreed to marry Romeo and Juliet, he should've taken the responsibility for this action. He should've informed their parents and reconciled them to the marriage instead of leaving Romeo and Juliet to fight for themselves in Limbo.*

*When Juliet confronts him about her forthcoming marriage to Paris, he doesn't ask for God's guidance or consider approaching the parents to beg for their understanding and compassion. He acts as a man turning to his own talents in alchemy. The Friar's final human act is running out of the tomb leaving Juliet, at the sound of noise outside. He is aware of her desperation and yet he abandons her to her final deed.*

*Even in the final moments of this tragedy, he can't reconcile himself to the part he has to play. He can't accept the realization that you just don't walk in and out of people's lives whenever you feel like it.*

*"I am the greatest, able to do the least." It has taken the deaths of Romeo, Juliet, and Paris to make him understand this. It's too bad it didn't occur to him sooner.*


No longer in my Shakespeare course do I know what my students are going to say in their papers. One says that Mercutio dazzled everyone, including women. Another says Mercutio may be kidding Romeo about being in love because he himself is afraid of women. One says that Antonio, the merchant of Venice, seems unnaturally willing to give up his life for his friend Bassanio, who borrows money from him to court the rich girl Portia. So willing, says the student, that maybe the two are homosexual lovers—and the class is in an uproar. As we check out these possibilities, examining pertinent lines, we get into the plays in a way we never did when I was doing all the speculating.

And they talk. I taped some of the sessions. In a class studying *King Lear*:

JAN DETWHILER: Yeah, and we were talking. A lot of my friends are getting married now and my cousin is also engaged and my mother and I were discussing what would happen when one of us in the family gets married, and then I said, "You know it's really funny, I talk to my friends and they feel like old maids—and the girls are my age, twenty-one, by no means old," and she said, "Well look at it as the youth craze in our country. By the time you're twenty-six you feel old if you're not married. And everybody wants to be young." People who are past thirty—you know—they keep saying, you're over thirty, no attraction. But everyone wants to be young. The image is youth and vitality. And after you get older you begin to feel worse and worse about it, and it gets attention and real pressure in our society right now. And people want to be younger and they can't be and younger people are rushing toward getting older. You know we all want to be twenty-one. Now I'm there and that's no big thing. I can do everything legally now, but—(hooting laughter).

PROFESSOR: You meant "Now, for the first time—"

JAN DETWHILER: Yeah. In *King Lear* they knew it was there but they felt they couldn't do anything about it. When the older people recognized the generation gap they sort of folded their hands and said there's nothing I can do about it. King Lear didn't want to go to Cordelia. Gloucester would just as soon jump off the cliffs of Dover rather than find Edgar. (Laughter.) But the younger people, including Cordelia—they went trying to bridge this gap all the time. But the thing is that they didn't tell their parents. We won't let them know we're trying to do this because it might bother them. And the older ones are trying to help the younger ones by dropping out of the scene. And that's why you have such a mess for a while because everybody would like to help everybody else but no one's telling them.

PROFESSOR: I like to talk about this subject because there are no easy answers. But Lear finally gets with Cordelia, doesn't he? He's finally able to talk with her.

JAN DETWHILER: My mother was saying last week and I didn't notice it until this weekend so much but my grandmother acts like King Lear. She was going on about something and then she was telling how hurt she was. Every day she got up and thought of how hurt she was because there weren't any grandchildren named after her. "And I just think about that every day," she said, "about how hurt I am. Now on that last grandchild, I didn't hint any more. I came right out and asked them to name that child after me and they wouldn't."

PROFESSOR: What's her name?

JAN DETWHILER: Her name's Cora. (Laughter.) But she wanted them to name her middle name. She said, "Now someone was named after my husband, and someone was named after the other set of grandparents," and she said, "and no one was named after me. I think about that every day." So I just started kidding her because I noticed how much she was acting like King Lear and I said, "Oh dear, she's going to write us out of her will," and she said, "Oh, I'll give you the whole will if you'll name your first child. . . ."

To bring about such a discussion I had to get some of the students to commit their experience and thoughts to that moment. They had to place a part of themselves before all of us, to open up, to *make themselves vulnerable* to Shakespeare, to the other students, and to me. [For a parallel use of *vulnerable* by a working anthropologist, see Denis Goulet, "An Ethical Model for the Study of Values," *Harvard Educational Review* (May 1971, pp. 205-227).]

In my first three years as a college student, I felt vulnerable most of the time, but it was a vulnerability based on fear and weakness. I felt as if I were strapped to a chair, being questioned by the police. In a few moments my guilt would be revealed. No doubt about the crime. It was being enrolled in that college in a state of ignorance. It was not knowing the answers to the questions. I might get by the first or second question, but I could not hold out. The professor was always more learned than I—maybe not in everything, but we were talking his subject. The course was his subject. He had specialized in the damned thing and had a doctor's degree in it. My crime was to exist in a state of relative ignorance and there was no way of finding redemption as long as I kept taking that course.

□

    I said to Joyce Tiefenthal Macrorie the other day (I hate to call her "my wife," a term that makes her sound· like a material possession) that in this new way of teaching I get a sense of power from seeing students exercise their powers, not from my keeping myself up and them down, but rather from my inducing them to make themselves vulnerable to the materials and disciplines to be learned, to me, and to each other. And from my becoming vulnerable to their experience and thoughts. It is not, I said, the old power game.

    Joyce replied that when my students do well that makes me more powerful, that my reputation is enhanced by their success; so I am in fact gaining power when I teach them to do well. I have to admit she is right. Throughout this book I have said "my students." I have not devised a way of eliminating all the negative effects of gaining power. As Joyce said, "If students learn something through your method, they are changed as persons, made more powerful, but they may still feel beholden to you."

    "If they go on to teach others better than I do, I would feel fine."

    "No," she said, "you probably would be jealous."

    Someone in the learning situation always holds the inferior position, and that someone is the student. Inevitable, I found myself thinking. But in this new way the superior-inferior relationship is lessened because the teacher makes himself vulnerable to his students' experience. He profits from them. No matter how thoroughly he has thought through his discipline, his students bring to the experience of his field or subject unique facts and thoughts that change his thinking.

    But Joyce is right. Those of us teaching in this new way, or other ways counter to the traditional, have not discovered a leaderless method. Some nondirective teachers and counselors deceive themselves into thinking they have. But power remains a prize we cannot help reaching for. The woman or man who calls the class together or advertises she is available to learners is by those acts making herself the leader, and students are aware of that. She and they may want to forget that, but they cannot, except momentarily. Some of those moments are happy and successful, some sad and disastrous.

    Yet I cannot consider this kind of teaching exploitative. The good feeling I have when my students experience a good feeling from performing strongly may have in it elements of mastery or power, but it is far up on the positive end of the scale from the feeling I have gotten in the past from showing off my knowledge.

    The new method of enabling described in this book is based upon encouragement of a person for doing valuable work. It is not "positive reinforcement" administered to a slave working in a diamond mine. When a student does not respond to encouragement and does not attend class regularly, a teacher probably cannot make the course work for him. But until the last moment he should be trying to encourage him.

☐

Tonight, reading James Boswell's *London Journal* and thinking of the way Jamie recorded thousands of things Dr. Johnson said and did —so many that Boswell took six years to sort through all those treasures when he was preparing to write Johnson's biography—I thought: I have written a rare book about college teaching. Not a series of generalizations occasionally interrupted by a short, sharply remembered moment, but a record of the life of a number of classes. I don't recall ever reading a book like that by a professor. How could I have furnished my readers such detailed accounts? I did not keep a daily or weekly journal. What enabled me to do that were the files I had made of student writing. I simply kept the master stencils of all the work I reproduced for class discussion. No matter how foolish or stupid or forgetful I have been as a teacher in the last eight years, the work of many of my students at many different moments was worth their attention and mine. Much of it proved memorable. When I came upon these files, dozens of pieces of work called up for me the circumstances of their making and their reception by the class, and I was back there in Room 3325 or 1112.

Until he becomes master, a learner is apprentice. Preparing himself. But the work of an apprentice can be sound and useful. Only the narrowest, most egotistic master drives out of his apprentice all his humanity, his uniqueness. In a great school—whether it be an educational institution or a maestro's workshop—the apprentice experiences masterful moments. It is not all rote and drudgery.

Like the best life, the best school combines polarities. Discipline, discipline, discipline; and freedom, freedom, freedom. The wisdom and craft of the past brought up against the pressing present. But in that last phrase I have spoken no more than the creed of the established education that has held back young persons for thousands of years. The opposite must also occur: the newly discovered truth and craft of the present must be brought up against the formidable past.

The reason that we teachers have seldom generated a spark between these poles is simple. In our classrooms we have denied our students their lives.

Chapter 2

# The Divine Right of Scholars

□

The true scholar grudges every opportunity of action past by, as a loss of power. It is the raw material out of which the intellect moulds her splendid products. A strange process too, this, by which experience is converted into thought, as a mulberry leaf is converted into satin. The manufacture goes forward at all hours.

"The American Scholar," Ralph Waldo Emerson

Customarily I now ask students to look at whatever we are studying with their own eyes before they turn to the judgments of critics or practitioners in the field. And to check their perceptions against those of the other students and me.

In the days when I used to lecture in my Shakespeare class, students used critics as crutches and looked anywhere they could to find support. A number wrote something like this: "In those days they believed in the divine right of kings, so Richard II naturally felt he had to hold onto the crown. It had been given him by divine right." I would bring up the statement in class and wait, hoping someone would say that Richard didn't always appear to want to be king. But no comment. They had read the play through a screen of half-understood historical knowledge. I would try to persuade the class that the play was a complex study of a man who felt ambivalent toward the crown. But it was a hard go. In high school many students had been taught that people in "the olden days" believed that kings were divinely appointed. If several characters in the play mentioned "divine right" that was what everyone believed in that time. No student stopped to consider that if Bolingbroke deposed King Richard, he at least must not believe that all kings were divinely appointed. That is the way the Test-Grade institution affects persons. I have seen the same thing in youngsters who go to elementary school to lose their minds.

In contrast, Diane Melger, one of my students in a recent Shakespeare class, read the play and made this entry in her notebook. Like much of the student writing in this book, it has not been edited by the writer or me.

*We do in our day have an example of the divine right of kings. Although not a king, the Pope of the Catholic Church is deemed infallible—hinting at being close to divinity or divine right. For 18 years I thought the Pope was infallible, until one day I read that somewhere around 1865 a group of Cardinals decided that the Pope was infallible.*

*Well, if ordinary men (and yes, for the believer and the nonbeliever a Cardinal is a man) could decide that the Pope was to be infallible from that time on, I guess to me that was proof enough that the Pope, in fact, too, was an ordinary man, created and loved by God as man—not near-God. Well, during all those years of thinking the Pope was infallible, I also thought that concept of divine right of kings was a little beyond belief. To think that anyone would believe such a thing.*

*Not seeing myself in any situation at all similar, I felt free to ridicule such ideas. The fact that in* Richard II *there were people like me (both "before" and "after") and that there was unrest and finally an overthrow, can also be brought to today. For my age group, the question of birth control (I am definitely talking about Catholics) is a debatable, if not revolutionary, subject—and the Pope is losing his infallibility, just as Richard II lost his divine right. (Even before popes were decreed infallible there must've been an inner sacred feeling that he was in the hearts of many, many Catholics.) Disgrace is brought to many Catholics and perhaps to the Church as various "human" actions are happening within the Catholic Church. Disgrace came to Richard II, too, for his many wrongs. His being inhuman and insensitive brought all this about. The same can be said about the Catholic Church—it is finally beginning to look at the "human" side of things and is paying in many ways for its inhuman ways in the past. Institutions should not always be inhuman and neither should kings and other leaders. (By "human" and "inhuman" I don't mean "civil" or "torturing"—I mean the very quality of "humanness.")*

Diane Melger was a scholar in the "right state" as Ralph Emerson put it—"Man Thinking." (He should have said "Person Thinking.")

Frequently the students who come to my classes with the highest grade-point averages are the least able to think for themselves. If they have become professionalized, already sailing on the voyage toward the M.A. or Ph.D., I shudder, for they have much to unlearn. In my last Shakespeare class, during the third week, I received this paper from a girl I shall call Dorothy Miner:

*What kept occurring to me while reading* Hamlet *was how much deliberation had gone into the interpretation of the play. How many scholars, literary greats, lovers of Shakespeare and plays pondered the numerous questions and riddles over the story. Did Shakespeare mean for his stories to be deliberated upon? Did his audiences go into so great a depth when they viewed his tales? Were they meant to? Did they have the capacity to do so? I seriously doubt it. Though in our classroom the history of Shakespeare's time is played down, it does have a profound bearing on the possible translations of his stories.*

*It seems important that the ability of the average frequenter of Shakespeare's plays (of his own century) as in comparison to the play attender now is considerably inferior; therefore would it not be conceivable that he would try and make his tales as simple and clear as possible? The many underlining themes in* Hamlet *must be made understandable for his contemporary audiences. The crowd that was attracted (or at least a goodly number) went to the Globe Theatre to be entertained not [to have] their intellects taxed. I am sure a person who goes to see animal fights will not continue to go to the theatre to become culturalized. That was not*

Shakespeare's main objective nor certainly was his audience's pleasure. The people of Shakespeare's era were born into a certain class and brought up in that distinction. There was no movement amongst classes; in other words they knew their place in society and kept to it. Could it be that Shakespeare is considered such a great writer because (for one reason) he serves two purposes? He could retain the attention of the lowly commoners of his day, entertain them, while at the same time be deep enough for his fans to delve into him and interpret him even today. Possibly the controversies surrounding his works are formulated only now by contemporary readers (i.e., in the last couple of centuries). Maybe we all try too hard to find the hidden meanings in the great work of this literary genius. There seems to be too much time devoted to trivial and unnecessary questions. His speeches, particularly his soliloquies, once the reader is able to fully understand the slang of the time, should be taken for face value (unless there is an obvious difference in the tone of the speech). That is how they are meant to be comprehended.

Shakespeare displays such magnitude in his comprehension of human nature and its abilities and failures and reactions. He writes what people are concerned about, problems that they understand: death, fate, God, destiny, all the universal truths. The characters in his tales are real human beings and he attributes to them traits that all can relate to.

Although Dorothy didn't know it, she was trying to sound scholarly and profound. Her paper is a swamp of contradictions. The average frequenter of Shakespeare's theater was stupid, but Shakespeare was possibly great because he wrote for the "lowly commoners" as well as his perceptive "fans of today." But maybe we perceptive fans "try too hard to find the hidden meanings in the great work of this literary genius." Hamlet's soliloquies, for example, "should be taken for their face value. That is how they are meant to be comprehended." This was early in the class. By the end of the semester Dorothy had learned to look at what was in front of her and judge on the basis of her own observations and the other students' responses to the plays. She saw that she was perhaps one of the lowly commoners who might miss a subtlety in Shakespeare. The subtleties multiplied, including those in Hamlet's soliloquies, and paid off in meaning after meaning beyond their "face value" when she pondered them.

I want students to learn to move back and forth between people of another time and theirs and illuminate both, as Dorothy Miner did not want her fellow students to do. That Elizabethans baited bears does not tell me any more about how they took Shakespeare's plays than that a few American soldiers—like their North Vietnamese opponents—cut off the ears of their dead enemies. Both facts speak our gross humanity. But the tradition of arrogance is so strong in our scholarship that a teacher must set many of his students on a new course before they can make past and present speak to each other.

I was not dismayed when Dorothy introduced her doctrine of superiority into our class. Apparently I had made myself vulnerable enough even in that class that she felt free to attack a strongly stated warning I had made early in the class—Watch out for using history as a guide to reading Shakespeare's plays.

In the past my students were fond of saying that the Elizabethan audience must have included a lot of low, coarse persons because Shakespeare employed considerable bawdy language. I now tell my classes that when I went to see *The Taming of the Shrew* performed to a university audience in about 1966, I witnessed this response. Petruchio hoisted Kate on his shoulder, presented her backside to the audience, read a bawdy line accented with gesture, and the educated spectators lost control of themselves in raucous laughter. The action on stage had to be suspended for thirty seconds. This is an old story in the world: the country club set complaining about the vulgar "Them" who live by the railroad tracks, then going off to a drinking party where the game is to tell the longest "dirty joke." Dorothy had a long way to go before she understood that Shakespeare, like Chaucer, did not and could not use the Puritan epithet "dirty" before the word "language." Or that a reader could find that out by studying the plays better than by reading history books.

The paper I received from Dorothy Miner is one I meet rarely in my classes these days. When their own experience and thinking are taken seriously by other students and me, my students habitually ask honest questions of what they read. They exhibit a naiveté that impels them and relaxes me and their fellow students. Nowadays I find myself questioning most received opinions, but not as I did when I was a college student. Then I came home to mock my middle-class family and friends. Now I question the most revered scholarly opinions not, I hope, to show my superiority, but because I know that schoolmen are as likely as anyone else to be blind or impractical. I see, for example, that the doctrine of the Divine Right of Kings must have been another creation like the Monroe Doctrine. They were both attempts to give authority to the selfish protection of power: to help a king stay on the throne, to help the United States Government keep its dominance in Central and South America. Counters in the power game, not beliefs at all.

☐

Once my students found their innocence and insouciance in reading Shakespeare's plays before someone else's ideas, I began to go their way too. I thought about some of the major scholarly statements, for example, E.M.W. Tillyard's *The Elizabethan World Picture.* The very title made me tremble when I first heard it. The man must know so much to talk about the whole Elizabethan world picture. I went back to the little book the other day. Mr. Tillyard talks of the Great Chain of Being (angels down to oysters) and other notions or metaphors of cosmic order. He says that "this idea of cosmic order was one of the genuine ruling ideas of the age . . ." and adds that "the pictures of civil war and disorder" that Shakespeare's history plays present have "no meaning apart from a background of order to judge them by." He argues that the ordinary educated Elizabethan lived with these ideas in his mind. He may have; I have no way of knowing; I think Mr. Tillyard doesn't either. To say to what extent an idea permeated the lives of men living in any age in the past is one of the most shaky of enterprises. We have seen in our time that the once-accepted notion of slaves in America being happy-go-lucky is a distortion. There were many slave insurrections, as we have learned recently. Even today, what percentage of Blacks are militants and what percentage "Toms" is unknown—and to those of us living at this hour, not four hundred years later.

The American tag line that all men are created equal appears in many books, newspapers, documents, even carved in brass and stone in contemporary America, but does that mean the notion is "one of the genuine ruling ideas of the age"? No, but it might be said that many laws on the book suggest that men are more often treated equally here than in most other countries. Other laws show that men as individuals are not treated equally with corporations. News reports demonstrate that that the poor go to jail more often for the same crimes than the rich, etc. The American notion of equality is a slippery matter and I would hate to write about it four hundred years from now.

For his proof Mr. Tillyard turns to the only possible sources: written accounts, most of them literary or religious. That a lot of medieval or Elizabethan writers used metaphors of cosmic order Tillyard can easily point out, but he does not demonstrate that Shakespeare's histories have a great deal more meaning once one is familiar with the terminology of order. Nor does he show that they have "no meaning apart from a background of order to judge them by." His is a paradigm of scholarship: it is a highly condensed presentation of a highly abstract view of intellectualized relationships between man and his spiritual and earthly environment. It quotes a wide range of Elizabethan and medieval sources. Its schemes are detailed and hard to follow. Reading it makes one feel erudite; the references and vocabulary are elevated. I can hear Dorothy Miner telling me that one simply can't read Shakespeare's plays without Tillyard. I suspect that the whole matter is so much more complicated than Tillyard's 109-page book implies—that to understand a little part of it well would be to open up one's understanding of man tremendously. How was this doctrine or imagery used in the real lives of persons? How wielded—as all doctrines are—in the power struggles of the time? I want Mr. Tillyard and other scholars, having once found a doctrine in the past, to bring it up to the present and see it through contemporary parallels. And to analyze the contemporary parallels through it. I hope that we turn back so we will enrich our present lives. Mr. Tillyard made a small attempt to do this, but his thrust comes from past materials pitifully fragmentary.

The sparseness of evidence in Tillyard's book makes me think of a scholarly work that meant a great deal to me as a college senior years ago, Caroline Spurgeon's *Shakespeare's Imagery*. Miss Spurgeon catalogued all the images used by Shakespeare (as if she were a human computer in the pre-IBM age) and showed his wide knowledge of the natural and man-made world. His memory of the names of things in the world is itself remarkable, but what he did in composing active images with them is staggering. Also, Miss Spurgeon showed that most plays were dominated by images from one or another topics—like flowers, illness, war, or whatever. For the most part she stayed down on the level of the things, but when she made her guesses about Shakespeare's attitudes they were more exciting and compelling than most scholars' because based on so many particulars which lay before the reader.

Spurgeon's book does not continually refer to or print other writings, and in that sense I suppose it is not the purest kind of scholarship. It does not read like conventional student work, always leaning on someone else, until the body and voice lose their vitality.

I know how simplistic my remarks here may strike some scholars. I hope what I say is naive. Increasingly I find the commonplace jokes about the academy just. We professors live in ivory towers; we get lost in terminology; we become digesters of what has already been digested a hundred times. We need to make ourselves vulnerable, like babies learning to walk. We need to encourage students to become vulnerable by introducing their real feelings and thoughts and experience into our classrooms. We are the thinkers, the detached observers, who should be able to see where the "lowly commoners" are taking themselves and us. But we have seldom sensed what it is like to live out there. We believe we can achieve absolute objectivity because we are already living and working on a higher level than others.

Recently a leader in the English profession asked me to join a national committee which would play watchdog on government and business workers and administrators who use words deceptively. I could not join because I believe we professors have no ground on which to stand while watching the other unconscious liars. We promise in our college catalogs to make independent thinkers of our students—by tests, corrections, term papers, and closed-circuit television. And we talk of the sanctity of the individual.

In my earlier remarks I did not mean to suggest that Professor Tillyard's *The Elizabethan World Picture* is a fraud. It is a proper exercise of scholarship. He took an idea developed in a long book by Arthur O. Lovejoy called *The Great Chain of Being* (1936), focused it on Shakespeare and other Elizabethans, extended the Chain to include a set of correspondences and a dance, found some more references to it in literature and theology, and pointed out some passages in Elizabethan writing that are illuminated by a knowledge of his conceptual structure. I found that his book seldom helped me read the passages he cited. In discussing Shakespeare's *The Tempest* he says, "Trinculo and Stephano are low in the scale of humanity. Caliban is largely bestial, a better log carrier than a man and perhaps of cruder appetites, strong too in fancy in which according to one Renaissance theory beast excelled man . . . yet in the end he shows himself incapable of the human power of education." I think what Mr. Tillyard has said here obfuscates Shakespeare. Anyone capable of reading *The Tempest* all the way through sees that Trinculo and Stephano are vulgar and that Caliban is bestial. One does not need a Great Chain of Being to place them on. What is exciting is the character given them, the buoyancy and lightness of creatures brought alive—once more the fullness of Shakespeare's acceptance of the world. However limited or outcast, the wit of this beast Caliban, the wit of the gravedigger in *Hamlet*, the beleaguered Jew in *The Merchant of Venice*, and the bastard in *King Lear* shows us they are intensely alive and worthy of our attention as individuals. This is what Shakespeare and Chaucer bring to us in large measure. E. M. W. has tilled a standard scholar's yard (Shakespeare's John of Gaunt would have liked such crude punning) and found some small plants. I doubt that he would claim much for his performance. He had set out, he said, to write a long book on Shakespeare's history plays and this one became an offshoot. I think it might better have been published only in a scholarly journal so that professors could not so easily require it for their introductory Shakespeare classes. But I understand why some do. We English professors would all like to find some scheme that would light up Shakespeare for our students while keeping us in the position of being the explainers of arcane lore.

The effect of assigning scholarly studies like Tillyard's to students is often to keep them away from Shakespeare's plays, not only because it is something else to read which will eat up their limited time (pressed as they are cramming for tests, writing interminable term papers, and reading ten books for the Modern Novel course), but also because it pushes them to read any passage about angels or man's place in the world first as an example of what Tillyard has said and second as a speech by a character in a certain play. Man does not live through books alone. When Hamlet says,

O heaven, a beast that wants discourse of reason
Would have mourn'd longer.

his impulse is human. Without any knowledge of the Great Chain of Being, you or I might have said that if we found our mother marrying a month after our father's death. Usually the natural (as opposed to intellectual) comes first. The man who encountered the primal dog found out quickly that the beast could not reason so well as he. It is natural that we call people we despise "dogs" and then go home to treat our dog better than our child. One does not need to study theology to appreciate this paradox. Yet after Mr. Tillyard quotes the above lines from *Hamlet*, he says:

> . . . the whole context is there. The apostrophe to heaven is more than mere interjection and is meant to bring in man's celestial affinities. Reason, man's heavenly part, has been degraded and he has sunk lower than the beasts themselves. Gertrude's sin is not against human decency alone but against the whole scale of being.

Oh yes, maybe so. Maybe not. When I hear of the latest atrocity in my time—a Vietnam village napalmed, a policeman gunned down while walking his beat—I find myself asking what sort of creatures we are. Hamlet is such a thrilling human being because he is forever moving from precipitate action to reflection upon its consequences and upon the place of man in the world. But I have found him such by reading the plays many times, not by reading *The Elizabethan World Picture*.

☐

One day in that last Shakespeare class I taught, Patricia turned up with a standard literary paper in which she said she had read a critic who pointed out Shakespeare's heavy use of the word *nature* and his frequent mention of natural elements. She had noticed this, too, she said, particularly in the storm scenes. She had no questions about it and no further point to make, merely wanted to share the observation with the class. I was disturbed. A person who had been so intuitive in comparing her emotional life with that of Juliet and Hamlet but had concentrated too much on hers so she didn't always communicate the parallels, now had flipped over to the other side and borrowed a scholar's notion without doing anything with it. Again no commerce between the objective and subjective. I suspected she might have written the paper as a swipe at me for restricting her talk about herself in class. "O.K., if you don't want to hear about me, I'll give you the standard meaningless stuff."

I brought up her point in class, hoping that another student would find something for us in Shakespeare's emphasis on nature. When no one did, I told a story of my own.

In 1966, when a great snowstorm hit Michigan, Joyce and I tried to drive home from the university but went off the invisible road and had to abandon our car. We had before us about a mile and a half—

maybe two—to walk to our country home through snow drifted knee and waist high. We stopped at the first house we came to and phoned our girls, then nine and six. They had returned on the school bus earlier. They were happily playing in the snow. Everyone else in the area, according to the radio, felt Death was stalking them. Coming out of that house, Joyce slipped in a snow bank and sprained her hip. No cars could use the roads between us and our house. We set out again, I pushing something of a path for her with my knees and feet. I thought of carrying her but knew I couldn't drain my energy that way and still keep walking. She said, "For the first time in my life I feel the possibility that I may die if I can't keep going."

I kept reassuring her we could reach another house before she gave out and that there was no such possibility. We walked on, the white stretching out, covering low bushes, standing against the trunks at a level I had never seen before. No road where there had always been a road. No car noises. Such an effort to lift one foot and put it down. And time had gone wrong. We had been walking for an hour and a half and had traversed about three quarters of a mile. We seemed stuck in space. We began to talk in a new way, at one moment complaining angrily at our pain and exhaustion, at another speaking peacefully, our senses sharpened by the changed world. I think we were feeling love in a foreign way. The slight possibility of dying made us value each other more highly. Tired as I was I could feel myself reserving energy to do whatever might be necessary to get Joyce to safety if she could no longer walk. I knew then what she meant to me.

We made it back to our house. I told the story to the Shakespeare class—not saying anything about our feelings of love, which did not occur to me in that exposed place—and said that before that time I had never understood how Lear might have been transformed by living through the storm on the heath with Poor Tom and the Fool. If no one in Lear's social and political world had been able to show him by act and word how selfish he had been, I did not see how a storm could do it. I had read scholars saying that Shakespeare's use of nature in these scenes could be understood only by seeing the natural elements as symbolic of his inner change. They praised this projection, which they assumed to be entirely metaphorical. And some discussed earth, air, fire, and water and the medieval "beliefs" about them. I thought, "O.K.," but I was a little resentful. Seemed to me the play was highly realistic in other parts and that Shakespeare's triumph was that he had presented such extremes of human emotions believably. So the more they argued, the less I thought of the play.

□

Recently I had another experience like that of the snowstorm. This time it was ice that visited my country place, such a storm that thousands and thousands of trees lost branches in the area that I travel every day to get to my job. On the second icing night, I was out on the long private road which goes to my house, sawing and chopping at limbs that obstructed the road and hung down cold and heavy and jangling, brushing my face. Small pieces of wood and ice rained on my head. As my energy dissipated, I grew desperate and began to flail. Every minute or two I heard a great report like a giant rifle in the woods, sometimes near, sometimes far: a branch or tree splitting. I wondered there in the dark whether the next one would occur above me. I pulled on a small branch I had felled—heavy as a tree, loaded with half an inch of ice on every twig. Misting and freezing occurred at once. My cap was brushed off and my hair became wet. In the blackness I fumbled for it and wondered where I was. I had not purposely courted madness: I had to clear the road so I could drive to school the next day.

When I came down the hill that night I felt exalted. I had spent an hour and a half somewhere else, and yet I knew I had stood on my own familiar property. Tired in body, I came into the house and looked at everything there, including the ideas that had been working in my head for the last few weeks, freshly.

I am sure Shakespeare borrowed some of the symbolic machinery of his day when he gave King Lear words about the storm and his condition in it. But I am also sure that he wanted to show that a cataclysmic physical event has the power to cleanse a man of petty, worldly burdens. So many scholarly comments on a great writer reduce his characters, turn the reader to the architecture of abstract thought, and prevent us from seeing ourselves and his characters deeply. Echoing in my head now are some of the many sudden comments of my students in Shakespeare. "Oh, I had an experience like that—" "Yeah, that's true. I knew a fellow once—" Then I see it as our job to look at the two experiences, the one in Shakespeare, the other in the student's life, and see how they are alike and different. My wife was not changed by the snowstorm or I by the ice storm so much as Lear by his storm. We had not treated our daughters as he had his, but in comparing, we might have found more likenesses than we first imagined and we might have understood better what Shakespeare was saying.

If my reader goes along with what I have said here he may think, "That's all very well, but a student must get there on his own in his own life outside the classroom. A teacher cannot endow him with perception and insight; either he is capable of that or he isn't."

But I am saying there is a progression here and it can properly be called a method. First, the teacher invites students to be truthful; second, they come to value their own experience and insights into it; and third, with that experience and insight they make themselves vulnerable to the experience the teacher introduces as the principal material of the course. Once I have induced half or more of the students in a class to do that it is easy to make myself vulnerable in the same ways. There are three bodies of feeling, thought, and action here: those of the students, mine, and those of the work before us. Each opens itself to the other.

I must add: in such an occurrence, what place is there for "A," "B," "C," "D," and "F"?

## Chapter 3

# Jesse Mack

☐

He dealt in ideas without seeming to do so; he led and guided with so gentle a touch that one began to think almost despite oneself. The process once started, he continued in such fashion as to instil into my very soul the determination to be a seeker after truth, the elusive, perhaps never to be attained, complete and utter truth, no matter where it led or whom it hurt.

[Edmund Wilson quoting Judge Harold Medina on his professor at Princeton, in "Christian Gauss," *A Literary Chronicle*: 1920-1950 (Garden City: Doubleday, 1956), p. 23.]

□

The other day in the university library, as I reached for a book, I heard a soft voice. "Mr. Macrorie!" It was Sandra Rotunda. She said she was still taking classes and I said I was writing about teaching and wondered if she had any idea why she and others in that Shakespeare class had been so reluctant to talk. She said, "I don't know" and looked puzzled. "I felt that probably what I would say would be trivial and most of what the other kids would say would be trivial, so I didn't talk much."

I said I believed I had put too much responsibility on the students for carrying the talk. She agreed. When I left her I thought how frightful for a girl that intelligent to fear she would speak trivialities. In two classsses I had listened to her talk occasionally. Always her comments seemed to issue from fresh-water springs.

That conversation with Sandra reminded me that in the first three years of college I never expected to learn anything from my fellow students. The line ran from the teacher in front of the room to me. Then another line ran from him to the student sitting next to me.

□

In high school I sat in a history course taught by Mr. G, a man my mother knew. Both at home and at school he had the reputation of being an intellectual with an acerbic sense of humor, a type rare in that isolationist little river city. We studied history—I don't know what it was now, maybe "Modern European," meaning the world seen from the White west—out of a textbook with those bold-faced headlined paragraphs: The Boer War. Covered in ten lines or so, seldom a whole page. And up there was smiling, round-faced Mr. G making what I supposed were subtle and humorous observations beyond the textbook. I didn't understand them. I didn't get the point of the Boer War if there was one stated or implied in the pseudo-objective textbook. Probably the teacher was developing some ironic point of view, but he came from another universe and did not know that he must let me bring my limited world into the classroom before I could get with his expanded one. So I studied the book, gave back the answers on the test, and got my "A."

I went on like that through high school and college (only it was "B" there and sometimes "C"), until I came upon Mr. Garvin in Ethics and Jesse Mack in Nineteenth-Century Romantic Literature. In that course Mr. Mack mis-estimated his audience. We students were going under a good bit of the time. I drowned fifteen or twenty times. Thinking of that course the other day I said to myself, "The vocabulary of the central book in the course was over my head." But I know now that the matter is never that simple. I can learn from books that contain words I do not know. In that class I was seldom swimming. I think suddenly of my favorite definition of schooling—"a swimming together." Mr.

Mack had not set up that class, as he had his seminars, so we students moved together.

I want to think about that class more particularly, for in design it was almost a great one. It was taught by the man who enabled me to write and think more than any other teacher I have had. Nineteenth-Century Romantic Literature. We started with the writings of William Blake and went on to those of Wordsworth, Shelley, Keats, Coleridge, and the others. We did not simply read them. We also bought and read a book called *Rousseau and Romanticism*, written in 1919 by a then celebrated professor of French literature at Harvard, Irving Babbitt.

Today, thirty-four years later, I have skimmed through the book. It is a learned, straightforward argument for the supremacy of the classic position over the romantic. I do not wonder that my memory of the book and course is clouded. In his third year of college, that young man from Moline, Illinois, was not ready for passages like this:

> The distinctions by which he [Kant] works out the supposed relationship between judgment and imagination are at once difficult and unreal. One can indeed put one's finger here more readily perhaps than elsewhere on the central impotence of the whole Kantian system. Once discredit tradition and outer authority and then set up as a substitute a reason that is divorced from the imagination and so lacks the support of supersensuous insight, and reason will prove unable to maintain its hegemony. [p. 42]

On rereading Babbitt, I find him brilliant but tiring. Except for citing a score of lines from Romantic writers and a few incidents from their lives, the book is philosophic—that is, it generalizes. I think Mr. Babbitt is sound in his views. Today his book makes a useful argument against those who uncritically espouse a life of instinct and spontaneity. I feel no love for him because in taking a position for both freedom and discipline (or received opinion) as I also do, he habitually scorns those who speak for freedom. I habitually scorn those who speak for authority.

But in my undergraduate days at Oberlin, I could be only frightened by such a book. I think I remember hating Babbitt for putting down the Wordsworth and Shelley I was coming to like. We spent a semester studying Babbitt's definitions of *Classic* and *Romantic*, apparent opposites. When we had finished we all agreed that often a work of architecture or literature considered Classic has a good deal of Romantic elements in it, and vice versa. I saw for the first time that such abstract definitions are man's inventions: he devises them for convenience, but the world out there is what it is regardless of them.

As I look back on that class I see its design as bold and useful: we were to read prose and poetry of writers customarily designated Romantics and use them to test the thesis of one of their major critics. Over four months we were to examine Babbitt's whole book and let him make his full case. We then would see a man who had been moved by a great range of work generalizing upon it. The intellectual at work. The breed that dominates the colleges and universities. What we students were supposed to become. Beyond these large considerations, Mr. Mack was using this book to hold together the numerous and diverse works of literature we were reading.

But it was not a right method for me, nor, I think, for most of my fellow students. Perhaps two or three were at home with such abstract thinking; though I do not remember anyone who seemed separated from the rest of us by his understanding of Babbitt. "Well," a reader may say, "how do you expect callow youth to learn to think abstractly until they are forced to follow an abstract thinker?" I expect them to learn to think abstractly by thinking abstractly, not by imitating someone else's most sophisticated performance. And I know they will do this best when they are thinking about their own materials. The poems and philosophy Babbitt was reacting to were familiar to him. He had made them his own. In Mr. Mack's class most of the works we read, as well as Babbitt's philosophical book, were new to us.

By their performance my students have taught me that if Jesse Mack was going to use *Rousseau and Romanticism* as a text, he should have first helped us understand a few of its central points. For example, he might have taken some of the Classical standards Babbitt cited (such as decorum and imitation) and some of the Romantic (such as spontaneity and primitivism) and let us apply them to things we cared for in our world. These might have been the Greek Revival architecture of the church on Tappan Square (built, as I remember, in 1839), the radical new offensive formation of the football team, or the irreverent new novel we liked. His principal job then would have been to exercise some classical restraint in letting us make our judgments, interceding only to point out whether in Babbitt's terms we were espousing the Classical or Romantic. He could have done this. He was one of the most patient teachers I have known. He respected students with an incredible depth of feeling for a man who saw so little impressive work from them in his regular lecture-discussion classes.

☐

I want to digress for a moment from Jesse Mack to think about Irving Babbitt's scholarly book. Irving Babbitt himself would have got through to us, and all his readers, more powerfully had he balanced his abstractions with experience drawn from life rather than books. In my last sentence I let myself put down the word *balanced* because I wanted to see it in its customary deceitful position. Then I could speak more precisely. For to connect one's abstractions and generalizations with experience is not to balance them. They are not disconnected things to be weighed against each other. They are organically related. The generalizations grow out of experience and the best ones are taken back ever to new and different experience to be tested and to breed new generalizations.

Babbitt says, "The imagination is supreme the classicist grants but adds that to imitate rightly is to make the highest use of the imagination" (page 69). This notion that the imagination of the Romanticist differs from the imagination of the Classicist is one of Babbitt's chief points. For him the one apparently is unrestrained and eccentric, the other has a controlled, moral quality about it which saves it from excess. It can operate while a person is imitating. Babbitt is fuzzy here. I want him to show his own imagination in action, perhaps both Classically and Romantically. But this is not his way. He criticizes the personal lives of Rousseau and other Romantics, and connects their immoralities with their espousal of Romanticism. Rousseau, he says, dilates on his "warmth of heart," his "keenness of sensibility," his "innate benevolence for his fellow creatures," his "ardent love for the great, the true, the beautiful, the just," on the "melting feeling, the lively and sweet emotion that he experiences at the sight of everything that is virtuous, generous and lovely," and concludes: "And so my third child was put into the foundling hospital."

Later Babbitt says that Rousseau "abandoned his five children one after another, but had, we are told, an unspeakable affection for his dog." I suggest, and without rancor, that Mr. Babbitt might have talked about his own relationships with children and dogs. I know that I often treat my dog better than my stepdaughters, but the reasons for my behavior are complex. An examination of some such weakness on Babbitt's part might have enlightened his judgment of Rousseau, might have taken him within what I call the Circle of Implication.

Like another fine book of its type, Joseph Wood Krutch's *The Modern Temper, Rousseau and Romanticism* analyzes a number of literary works from a special point of view and goes on both to state directly and to imply that its views may apply to all individual and social life—a better way to see the world and live in it. I admire such pragmatic concern. I recommend that writers like Babbitt and Krutch consider how persuasive their own experience may be to readers. And if they do not have at their disposal experience that bears out what they are saying, then they will be less sure of their conclusions, or perhaps decide not to publish the conclusions until experience has tested them. I seem to be speaking against all speculation. I do not mean to be. We must move forward, we must exercise what I think Mr. Babbitt says is our imagination. But even speculations are more compelling if a reader is allowed to see the experience out of which they arise.

This suggestion that scholarly books should arise more out of the writer's experience will sound naive to many readers. It is this naiveté that I wish to put to work. I have gained it from watching my students do things which the system has trained me to believe impossible for them. I can hear an opponent say that scholarly books are by their nature critical and generalizing, that they would be too long if they incorporated a great deal of firsthand experience. But whether a work is long or short, or should be published in smaller parts, is not the first question: What is its usefulness? I think *Rousseau and Romanticism* is provocative and exciting although it was almost incomprehensible to me when I was twenty, and it dragged for me when I was fifty-three. It is clearly written, not warm, but occasionally humorous. It employs considerable knowledge without being pretentious. It touches matters that are pertinent right now and will never become trivial. And yet I doubt it was highly influential or had a large sale beyond libraries. It probably did not persuade any Romantic poets to enlarge or discipline themselves. And I doubt that it influenced many other readers to balance their lives. I can hear the standard rejoinders, "But books don't reform people!" "The very nature of the university is to remove itself from the pressures and claims of everyday life and allow scholars to reflect upon what mankind is doing." I say if the reflection creates no more than an intellectual history or a log of critical differences, then why subsidize it? Henry Thoreau's *Walden* is a book. Malcolm X's *Autobiography* is a book. I think both have changed men's ways. As a result of reading Thoreau many persons have got up the next morning and gone for a walk in the woods and never stopped walking. As a result of reading Malcolm X some white persons have understood why Blacks they don't know stare at them with hostility. No longer puzzled, they can relax a little; and one of these years a relaxed white man perhaps will accept a black neighbor instead of spending his energy trying to make him feel like an intruder.

Any attachment may weaken detachment, and vice versa. But scholarship is ridden with the diseases of detachment; it has built up too much immunity to attachment. It could go a long way in making itself useful to students and citizens outside school before it needed to draw back once again. A small example. Without the habit of testing literature by holding it up against his own life, the critic soon begins to explain what persons do in a book as examples of artistic device—until there evolves what one critic calls an "archetypal criticism." True, art is not life, and artists are as much influenced by the forms of art as the reality of human behavior. But few artists employ forms only to be formal. Most hope to increase our sense of life, sometimes our understanding, by creating what Susanne Langer called a *virtual life.*

In *Rousseau and Romanticism* (page 292), Babbitt says that the storm in *King Lear* is another instance of the Romantic melding of man and nature. He makes no nasty remarks about Shakespeare being a Romantic but he brings up the matter in the context of condemning Romantic writers for claiming a false sympathy between nature and man. I am reminded that when I told my Shakespeare class of the cleansing feeling I experienced in an ice storm, I had come to believe that King Lear in his storm experienced a humbling of his excessive pride that represented a full and genuine transformation in the last days of his life. I had experienced nothing that drastic myself. After I had said that to the class, one student wrote in her journal that Lear had indeed changed, but only slightly, enough to be kind to the Fool and Poor Tom out in the storm and to ask forgiveness of his daughter Cordelia. But, said my student, he was too old and senile to see his part in bringing on the animosity of his daughters Goneril and Regan and other persons in the kingdom toward him. She was right. For years I had allowed myself to overstate the case. A storm had not completely rejuvenated King Lear or me, although it had had its effect. Attention to all the touchstones was necessary for me to see this: to a literary tradition, to an experience of mine, to the statements of my students who had closely looked at the play we were reading. To make myself vulnerable to all of these influences I believe was more enriching than to strive for a detachment I had been taught to prize as scholarly.

☐

Perhaps one of the reasons the man who used Babbitt's book as basis for his course was the most influential teacher I studied under was that he made himself more vulnerable to me than others did. Jesse Mack was a small man with a warm wrinkled face, never undignified, garrulous, or extroverted. I think he was intensely shy, realized not half the man he was. Yet the vulnerability did not arise from weakness.

By the time I was a senior I had come to admire and love him so much that I wanted to be with him as often as possible. He was another breed of man than I had ever known—not only thoughtful and learned but compassionate, humorous, and absolutely lacking in pretension. After the seminar in Eighteenth-Century Literature, which finished at four in the afternoon, several of us students would stop at the Campus Restaurant, which was on Mr. Mack's way home. There we would order old-fashioned sundaes served in a silver dish and topped with real whipped cream, the dark fudge steaming in a small green porcelain pitcher. One day when Alex Brooks, one of the frequent cohorts, was not there, Mr. Mack told a story about him. Alex had written a prize-winning study of migrant workers and gone out to Salinas, California, to see John Steinbeck, who had just published *The Grapes of Wrath*. I remember how Mr. Mack chuckled when he described Alex's visit. "He called up, you know, and was told that Mr. Steinbeck was not seeing anyone. So Alex immediately went to the ranch, knocked on the door, and announced himself to the man who opened it—Steinbeck. Alex said he knew a lot about migratory workers and began to prove it. Steinbeck could not deny the upstart and invited him in for lunch, during the course of which Alex in his usual way asked touchy questions.

" 'A lot of reviewers have praised your book, Mr. Steinbeck, but complained that the ending, in which the young woman gives her own milk to a starving man makes a maudlin finish.'

" 'Oh yeah,' said Steinbeck, 'they were probably all bottle-fed babies!' "

□

I am trying to remember my experiences with Jesse Mack because as a student I was a typical unread, nonthinking young man oppressed by grades and unable to make myself vulnerable to knowledge, the other students, or the teacher. What did he do that opened me? I took three courses from him, that first one in Nineteenth-Century Romanticism, a second in Shakespeare's Tragedies in the summer between my junior and senior years, and a third, a seminar in Eighteenth-Century Literature.

In the first course, as I have said, I was sinking in deep waters. One day he alluded to *Gulliver's Travels* and noticed that no one seemed to get his point. "Haven't you read the book?" he asked. Silence. "How many have read it? Raise your hands." About three hands in a class of twenty students went up. A few minutes later, he mentioned *The Odyssey* and the same thing happened, maybe seven hands. "This is incredible," he said. "You're almost all English majors and you don't seem to have read any of the classics. He took a poll of ten famous works and put his head down for what seemed thirty seconds. I thought he was about to faint, for he would never have overdramatized his feelings. About twenty minutes remained in the hour. He raised his head and said in the quietest but most trembling voice I have ever heard in a classroom, "Why don't you take off a few days and read some of the great books in the world?" He packed his briefcase and hurried out the door and we all sat there paralyzed by his violence. I went home, skipped classes all the next day, omitted lunch, and read *Moby Dick* from beginning to end. If he had reflected, he would not have been surprised that school had taught us not to read books. Surely it did not encourage us to read them because we wanted to or as if they were entertaining. Only as assignments, for the test. I am reminded of Sandy Rotunda's free writing at the beginning of that Shakespeare class:

> An assignment from a book is a cage. Success is a big cage comprised of little ones meshed together but each must individually be dwelt in. Encaged in a little cage. Even if the girl across from me now in the library does not want to roam the fields, she'd probably rather take a walk downtown, or sit at the union with some friends. Books are a higher pursuit, so she's scratching her ear and yawning.
>
> There's another girl doing the same. She was doing some frantic underlining. Driving herself to absorb, she's gotten tired. She's fidgeting with her eyes. The book is linguistics. Linguistics is a specialty for only special people. Yet if I had a linguist sit down and tell me about what he's doing, or even that girl—she probably would do more listening than fidgeting. Classrooms are not the place to learn. Books are a fantastic source of information

*when you need it. Or if you're in a discovery mood. But "reading"*
*to store information only is a dead process. It's already been stored*
*(info) because it's printed. Using it is something else again. Bore-*
*dom is the time lag of learning and doing.*

*I'm a fantastic storer. But doing, or the threat of having to do,*
*either makes my system race or stop for an instant. I'm not sure*
*which happens when you're suddenly frightened.*

*I hate to see people sitting over books. Since I spend most of*
*my time that way that's probably why I'm so frustrated. The*
*prospect of learning has always excited me. Yet I've always hated*
*school. Grace comes from discipline. Strutting from over disci-*
*pline. We don't know how to make people graceful, so they either*
*strut or slouch.*

Any book can become a grind when it's an assignment. I suppose the
suggestion that we students in Mr. Mack's class go home and read some
of the great books stuck in my memory because a professor had been so
moved that he had not finished out his hour. A sweet and gentle man
had gotten angry. He was suggesting that we should know something
not for a test, not as preparation for his class work; but so we could
share a knowledge of "the best that has been thought and said in the
world" as we tried to discuss another book.

☐

The moment that affected me most in all my higher education
occurred in Jesse Mack's Shakespeare class. I wrote the first paper on
*Hamlet* and got my "B," but came home every day excited by the life
in Shakespeare and Mr. Mack's ability to help me see its subtleties.
When we came to *Antony and Cleopatra*, I was enthralled. I sat home
reading to a friend, or to myself, line after line that gripped me. Cleopatra holding out her hand and saying "the hand that kings have lipp'd
and trembled kissing"—and I knew I would have expired had she held
it out to me. I had sense enough to recognize that Shakespeare had
pulled off the impossible in making these two the first lovers of the
world. He balanced their bragging imperial lines with gross ones like
these:

> ... rather on Nilus' mud
> Lay me stark nak'd, and let the water-flies
> Blow me into abhorring!

It was not melodrama: it worked on the highest and lowest planes. I
wrote a paper documenting how Shakespeare had made me believe in
this supercharged pair. I forgot to write dead academic prose. I thought
about what I was saying and collected my examples for over a week,

from radio and newspaper items, including Edgar Bergen's Charlie McCarthy, as well as from Shakespeare's play.

Although I listened intently to every word Mr. Mack said about the plays, I could tell that few of the other students found them as exciting as I did. When time came for handing back the papers on *Antony and Cleopatra*, Mr. Mack read mine to the class as a model of how to do the job. This was beyond all my hopes. If he liked it, it was good. He never praised a student's work unless he genuinely admired it. He was spare with words because he valued them. At the end of the hour when I passed his desk and received my paper, he said quickly, with a little smile, "Write more like this." I did. After that I wrote papers that counted for me and for the teacher, and in seminars for the other students as well. Mr. Mack knew I had written a raft of dull, verbose papers in the Romantic Poets course. He had let me know this was a breakthrough. A man I admired had encouraged me, not to study for a test or get the right answer but to use my mind and my resources.

At another moment he moved me with one remark. In the Eighteenth-Century Literature seminar in my senior year I had delivered a paper on the style of Edmund Burke. I can't remember now what the occasion was for my mentioning the Earl of Shaftesbury, but his name popped up in my paper as an influence on Burke. The paper seemed well received by the students and Mr. Mack, but before he turned to the next one, he said quietly, "Mr. Macrorie, you mentioned the Earl of Shaftesbury, but I didn't fully understand the role you said he played. Would you tell us a little more about Shaftesbury's influence on Burke, please?" I had borrowed a scholar's comment about Shaftesbury's influence, but I knew nothing of the grounds for his judgment. I squirmed. What could I say to bluff my way out? I had not one little fact with me to use. After an uncomfortable silence during which the whole class turned to see my response, I said, "I'm sorry, but I don't know a thing more about Shaftesbury."

"I see," said Mr. Mack in his gentlest tone. Then, as if he were addressing the other students rather than me, he added, "When you mention someone by name, you should know more about him than you say, or it is better not to mention him at all." I tried to follow that advice for the rest of my college years. Like every professor, I am still living through college years. I do not always keep faith with Mr. Mack's admonition but I know that my effort has improved the quality of my life.

Ever since those days I have considered Jesse Mack the greatest teacher I ever studied under. Why? Up until the day I found another way of teaching, the answer seemed easy. He had influenced me more than any other teacher. But now I see that in the Romantic Poets course he didn't teach me to write. And although he gave the encouragement in Shakespeare class that made some kind of writer out of me, he didn't seem able to inspire many students in the class that way. I worshipped the man. He was often a poor communicator, but always he said something he believed. He talked too low and fast to be always understood. His miniscule scribblings on our papers were almost illegible. After I had taken three classes from him, I helped other students decipher his foreign-looking script. But some of us were profoundly moved by him. He had what Aristotle called the most persuasive instrument a man can possess—an admirable character.

Jesse Mack was unassuming but terribly honest and hard on himself in his search for truth and understanding. I realize now that he made himself vulnerable. One afternoon we students sat in his seminar room for fifteen minutes past the hour waiting for him. No Mr. Mack. I would have waited until midnight, but after ten more minutes a fidgety girl with few brains walked out in the hall and phoned him. She returned and announced disdainfully: "He forgot!" Ten minutes later he arrived, puffing after a walking run of about five blocks, in good shape for a man over sixty. "Sackcloth and ashes, ladies and gentlemen!" he murmured as he slammed his books on the table. "Sackcloth and ashes. I was reading something, and I just forgot. It reminds me of a similar incident several years ago when I forgot a class. A girl called me up and read me out. She said she was paying good money for a college education and the least I could do was to show up for class." Everyone laughed with him as he picked up the papers to begin. Then he added, "She made Phi Beta Kappa that year."

The notion that Mr. Mack would ever not care about his teaching or about his students was so ludicrous to me that I could not seriously entertain it. At the Campus Restaurant with him we talked about anything that came to mind. I could see him tasting our conversation as if it were better than the hot fudge on ice cream. Once I remember he became excited when the popular music on the jukebox showed what he considered to be a clear derivation from Mozart. I'm sure he was right; his enthusiasm was proof. I didn't know Mozart at all. This was in 1939. I would have liked to have seen him relishing the derivations of rock music of the present time.

Several times he invited the class to his home for strawberry shortcake, once to hold the seminar, and once just for casual talk. One day I phoned him to ask if I could discuss a paper I wanted to write, and he said, "Come out right now. I'm just about to have late breakfast." After picking up some incredibly light French pastries and coffee in the kitchen, he took me up to his study. For many years his wife was invalided, but I never once heard him complain of having to do double work. He had no pretension about him, but lived well, savoring more aspects of life than I had dreamed of. I thought an intellectual man like a professor should be unremittingly austere. Once when I was crossing the street in front of the Oberlin bank, I met him in midpassage, while the light was still green. It was World Series time and he shouted as he passed, "Did you hear that double play that Joe Gordon pulled? Wasn't that remarkable?"

To me, an unsophisticated and puritanical youth from the midwest, the range in Jesse Mack was astonishing. He had a finely tuned sympathy with the arts of the eighteenth century and the Cleveland Indians, he kept beer in his icebox and wore sporty black-and-white shoes in the summer after he was sixty. Never has a year gone by in my life when I have not thought of him, and yet today as I write I believe I realize for the first time how much I have tried to model myself after him. The power of one man to affect another without ever saying, "Be like me."

The next year when the film *The Grapes of Wrath* came to Oberlin, I summoned all my nerve—maybe because I had Alex's example—and asked Mr. Mack if he would go to see it with me. He was surprised but apparently not offended, so we went together. I was thrilled as much by walking alongside my idol as by seeing the fine movie. When we left the theater, I could tell he was moved; and I was glad, for I felt the film was truer than anyone had a right to expect of Hollywood in those days.

As we walked the two blocks to his home, he said, "Henry Fonda was fine when he read the speech saying he would be wherever kids cried when they were hungry. Reminded me of Lear's speech 'Poor naked wretches—' " I agreed. I could see the parallel was just. I walked along a few steps gloating: a learned man was talking to me and I was understanding and making sense back to him. We were using our knowledge to discuss a movie! I had had no conversations like that back in Moline. I was present while a man was thinking, and not in a classroom. Only now do I see that this moment—so late in my education—probably moved me to begin making things I knew speak to things I was encountering for the first time. A sad comment on my schooling.

Thinking of Jesse Mack I remember a journal entry Nick Kekic made in my Advanced Writing class:

> *The concerned student should demand of the teacher: Show me the person you have made of yourself. Let me see its full size. For how can I judge what you know, what you say, what you do, what you make, unless in the context of the whole person?*

That is easy for a student to say, but as a professor I know how invaded I would feel if I let a third of the students in any of my classes get to know me as well as I knew Mr. Mack. I don't want them all poking around in my refrigerator for beer or arriving uninvited for a chat at dinnertime, and neither does my wife. I'm happy to be able to say that Mr. Mack would have helped me had I never visited his home or walked to a movie with him. The stage was his seminar in Eighteenth-Century Literature. Like his son-in-law, Andrew Bongiorno, who was the other great teacher I knew as a student, he knew how to make a seminar work. He let us choose our subjects, he took our papers seriously as we read them aloud at the big table in that dignified library room full of fine editions. And soon we began to take them seriously. He asked questions occasionally, sharpened the argument, but often talked less than one of the students. Two in that group of twelve habitually delivered weak papers. We learned to go easy on them. But the rest of us criticized each other's statements unrelentingly. The competition was intense, but not for a grade. We were trying to say something new to ourselves and to the persons around the table and make it stick. There were remarks about the style of our writing as well as the thought. If we wrote pompously, our words immanent in that quiet, charged room sounded awful. Next time we wrote with more restraint and honesty. Once a week, seven until nine. I remember bursting out of the library, out of that close room into the expansive air of a dark spring night, still riding the excitement of the talk and the criticism. Jesse Mack was the architect of those evenings, but they belonged to us, to Alex and Roger and me in a way that I had never dreamed possible.

I don't have to say that I regret Mr. Mack never knew how I felt about him; because a year after I graduated, I sent the president of the college a two-page eulogy of Jesse and asked that he transmit it to my old teacher. I don't have a copy of it, but I believe it was forthright and solid, as Mr. Mack had taught me to write by putting me in contest with my peers. He wrote back a simple, eloquent thank you.

Once after class waiting to ask Mr. Mack a question, I overheard another student say to him, "This course is killing me. I don't understand the assignments. Can't you tell me more about what I should do? I get home, read the book, and start to write my paper, and I don't know what I should say. There's a great high wall in front of me. I start climbing it but then I fall back. I climb again, same thing. I'm never sure what I should be doing, but I want to climb the wall."

"That's the way I want you to feel," said Mr. Mack with his sweet smile.

☐

Jesse Mack always spoke softly of his son-in-law, Professor Andrew Bongiorno, and with love. After I got to know Jesse at home, he would occasionally mention with pride his son Maynard, who was then on his way to becoming one of the most respected professors at Yale in recent times.

But I still have not answered my question—why was Jesse Mack the greatest teacher I ever had? To get help, I recently wrote several Oberlin classmates and his son, Maynard. Professor Arthur Eastman of the University of Michigan, known for his television programs on Shakespeare and other writers, wrote back:

I had Mr. Mack for one course—the Romantic Poets—and I recall that the assignments were long, that there were many papers, which I usually handed in late without suffering penalties, that the final examination contained an optional question for those who had time to answer it, and that students who attended a series of extra lectures Mack gave one afternoon a week on the 18th century background did not have to take the final. Mack was not a good lecturer, he mumbled and hesitated and generally threw away every possible opportunity for a climax or effect. What I remember was his presence, his face—the wrinkled kindliness of it, and interior melancholy, the gleams of quiet delight or subdued joy when one of us said something well or wise. He was himself a kind of saint, I suppose, his affection and his wisdom half inarticulate yet communicating themselves nonetheless.

Alex Brooks, a professor at Rutgers Law School, wrote:

I took Mack's Literature of the Bible course, which I enjoyed, but at which I didn't work very hard. When exam time came, the questions were mainly factual, rather than (as I thought they should be) concerned with literary issues, which I was prepared to discuss. So, instead of answering the questions, which I thought would have been a pointless and futile exercise in memorization, I made up ten examination questions to replace the ten questions Daddy Mack asked. He was quite taken with the audacity of it and gave me an "A" for the exam and course. I'm not sure I would have dared such a *tour de force* of examsmanship with other professors. But I knew he would understand and be responsive, even though it was a snotty thing to do. The story is more about a snotty young student than about a kindly and patient professor.

But I really produced for him in other courses. He taught, I think, by love more than anything else. He was far from a brilliant man. But he was so much in love with English literature and with being a professor that he communicated this love to his students who loved what he taught and loved him deeply. The seminar in Eighteenth Century English literature which you and I shared was one of the richest experiences I had at Oberlin. I will never in my life forget (and I can visualize it so easily now) Daddy Mack sitting at the head of the table smiling with such pleasure because the discussion was so serious, so good! Everyone worked for him, to the maximum of his capacity. One *couldn't* let him down.

Maynard Mack, Jesse's son at Yale, wrote me a few words about his father which make my old professor seem more amazing. My experience is that those of us who know our parents when we are adults see them stripped of most of their virtues, so that in our portraits they are foreigners to those outside the family who knew them. Not so with Jesse Mack, who seemed to his son very much as he did to his students:

> He would be simply overcome by the notion that an old student of his might trouble to write about him: you will remember how self-deprecating he always was. This it was, too, that kept him from writing for publication. I wouldn't know what those papers of his were like [I had mentioned two essays by his father I had read in manuscript] that he used to write once in a great while for (I believe) a "Cosmos Club." I know they always cost him agonies of introspection. It is perhaps one of these you have seen in the library. I suspect he never felt equal to writing for publication because he knew he had started late, was self-educated mostly, and was less interested anyhow in adding to the accumulation of knowledge than in discovering ways it could be made morally and artistically meaningful to men of good will. Though I never sat under him, this seems to have been his great gift. He made you feel that the bell tolled for *you*. And he was still more interested in *you* than what he was telling you. I wish I were more like him. He and my mother were lovely spirits from a world now mostly lost.

I hadn't known that Jesse Mack was mainly self-educated. Perhaps that accounts for part of his greatness: he never was finished by the schools.

Roger Garrison, who a few years ago was Vice-President of Briarcliff College in New York, found Mr. Mack as stimulating as I did, and he kept in touch with him over the years. He wrote me of Mr. Mack's last days:

> I visited him in the nursing home at Oberlin not long before he died. He was terribly emaciated and weak. His face was one mass of deep-graven lines; his arms and legs were as thin as reeds and streaked with purple veins and the brown blotches of old age epidermis. He lit up when he saw me in a way that I can't quite describe. There was, first, the look of recognition; then a struggle to attach the name to the face; and when I helped him by saying immediately who I was, he rubbed the back of his hand over his eyes and then reached the hand to me and put it over mine, saying how much it meant to him to have such a visit. We didn't

talk about much, really; but he did say one thing that I have not forgotten. "You know, Roger, it is not so bad when the body begins to break up and when the physical shell crumbles. But if I resent this state of mine at all, it is that my spirit feels insulted."

I believe this short account shows Mr. Mack's effect upon Roger as a writer. The description of the aged man is direct and almost brutal, but it serves to strengthen the later comments about spirit, which might seem sentimental without it. I think Jesse would have liked that description; it shows Roger's love for him was not soft.

*Chapter 4*

# A Free Class

☐

Freedom means essentially the part played by thinking—which is personal—in learning:—it means intellectual initiative, independence in observation, judicious invention, foresight of consequences, and ingenuity of adaptation to them.

John Dewey, *Democracy and Education*
(New York: The Free Press, 1966), p. 302.

☐

After I discovered a new way to teach, customarily I went to class prepared to be astonished—in Freshman Composition, Advanced Writing, Shakespeare, and Criticism of Mass Communication. I was confident, not that I knew my "subject," not that I would sound authoritative up there, not that no bright students would "pin me against the wall"; but that the persons in my class would frequently say and make and write things which would delight the rest of us, stick in our memories, teach us. I was not dreaming. I had the evidence.

I had learned from students that any human being at his best can illuminate some part of his interior or exterior world for others if he is both given freedom and challenged to take on discipline. Often the surest way to bring about high-level performance seemed to be to approach the act directly. For a long time I had felt that literature had been taught in a way that deprived the student of his own honest responses. And yet literature is itself a statement of personal, individual life—emotional, physical, intellectual.

At my university I had available what is called Senior Seminar, a course designed to give a small number of students, usually fourteen to sixteen, a chance to sit around a table and talk and write papers about a limited topic chosen by the professor and announced in a written description prior to course registration.

I wrote my prospectus for the course:

### NEW WAYS OF RESPONDING TO LITERATURE

Commenting on a piece of writing or a film so as to show what the work means to the reader as an individual as well as to the larger public. Students will be encouraged to do this in new forms—still pictures, slides, films, writing which parallels or opposes the work studied, created objects, or whatever. I mean the students will be speaking in these forms. They will be asked to confront the work of art with their own experience, in order to see both more precisely and fully; yet the course will not encourage them to value any damnfool thing they do or create just because it is their own. Discipline of many kinds will be expected. Goldie's admonition, "Just let it all hang out, ladies," will not be the motto of this course.

I was convinced that one of the reasons students of literature seldom make strong and perceptive criticisms of what they read is that they have few options. Often they must respond to what impresses them as watery pudding—for example Wordsworth or Whitman at their worst or Washington Irving at his most sentimental. Apparently the professor relishes the pudding or he would not be serving it up in such large helpings. In fact he probably assigns these readings because they are the proper diet for English majors—necessary if one is to *cover* American literature.

I knew that finally every good teacher of literature was trying to make perceptive readers of his students, not just introduce them to one *opus* or *corpus* or *genre*. I thought the lecturing and testing, the mouthing of criticism by professionals, all the tight assignments took away choices and thus reduced responses to the abstracted and the expected.

I walked into that seminar, said what I have just recounted here, and announced the first task:

"Take any piece of writing that has struck you lately. It doesn't have to be literature; a newspaper article will by contrast tell us something about literature. But take something you reacted to strongly, hated or loved or were shaken by, and write what you think about it. You may analyze it as you ordinarily do in a lit. class, but beyond that I want at least half the paper to present experience of your own that you believe has influenced your response to the work.

"Maybe your uncle was highly like or unlike a character in the work. Maybe you served in the army and the work is about military life. I'm not saying that every piece of writing affects you only as it touches your actual personal experience, or that your experience determines wholly what happens in the act of your reading it. On the contrary, any strong work establishes a life of its own. Reading it, you are taken into that life. Yet to some extent always your own life affects what you see there. Bring these two lives against each other.

"If you wish, you may make this statement in some other form than the usual critical essay. You may write a parallel work yourself, you may draw a picture, or present photographs or slides or films."

I had prefaced this assignment with my usual talk about speaking and writing truths and had handed out examples of phony, pretentious student writing. I also said a few words about what I thought made significance in art—the bringing together of two things that create tension and pay off in surprise. I invited the students to present thoughts about the matter themselves. I said that since so many young persons today were intrigued by film I would allow this class to consider pictures of all kinds as literature, or a form of art.

At that point a young man I later identified as Ben Whorl asked if he might say something that struck him as I was talking. He drew out a slide which we projected on the wall. It was a color shot of a plane, small, but lit clearly against a Pacific sunset. Ben said that for him this picture seen in the context he knew created the tension I had just talked about. Planes like this one returned to base every evening in the colored quiet skies after bombing and napalm raids that destroyed all the life in Vietnam villages. He made his comment briefly and modestly, and I could feel the class react, although only two students spoke up. I knew we were started in that class. A young man had presented a powerful work already, before the first assignment was to be handed in. Already my hypothesis had been proved valid.

□

I asked the students to skip the second meeting of the week so that they would have time to prepare their responses. A week later we met. One girl (I'll call her Ruth) brought a large drawing of a tree—adequate, but not compelling or memorable in my judgment, and the text of Joyce Kilmer's poem "I think that I shall never see . . ." as well as a poem she had written in contrast to Kilmer's. Her trees were not placid:

> *Trees whose boughs clutch at the sky*
> *Gnarled and knotted yet upward vie . . .*

She read both poems in a worshipful manner and the students looked round at each other and said nothing. I felt paralyzed. Maybe I had announced to the class earlier that I would allow only positive comments about student work for the first two or three weeks—I don't remember. Most of this class, which I taught less than a year from the time at which I am writing these lines, was a nightmare and my memories of it are limited and lurid. I waited. The students looked uncomfortable. Ruth, who had courageously volunteered to be first, and who during the first month of class was a welcome leader, looked dismayed.

Someone said, "I like the drawing of the tree." I waited for elucidation, but none came. If I remember rightly, one person said he thought the girl's poem was at least better than Joyce Kilmer's, and then we discussed that old chestnut tree which most of the students thought was sentimentally drawn. I added my condemnation of the tree which has a hungry mouth pressed against earth's breast and a bosom above that on which snow has lain. I was feeling better because some of the students were at least looking hard at Kilmer's squashiness. I was also feeling terrible because Ruth's considerable first effort had been almost killed by silence. In this course she could not now move from success to success.

□

Next Jimmy Gombara, who had read a poem by Galway Kinnell, volunteered. I believe he had not made copies of it for the class and we had a hard time remembering enough of it to discuss it. He had interspersed prose lines telling of his own closeness with a girl. He said they echoed the feeling of the speaker in Kinnell's poem. I was so confused by his presentation that I thought he had written some of the lines by Kinnell. Through his mumbled reading of the texts we did not have before us and my somewhat impaired ears, I got the feeling that his statement and Kinnell's about holding a girl they loved were valid, and that therefore he must have learned something in comparing them.

Ordinarily when I fail to hear clearly what a student has said or read across a classroom, the students sense this and help me out. But no help for anyone in this seminar.

As I remember, two students said they did not follow Jimmy's imagery in spots and one said he liked Kinnell's poem. But again the comments were grudging and appeared careless in the root sense of that word.

Next we looked at a paragraph by Jane Warn on her feelings about war. She supplied a poem by Rod McKuen, saying that some of his lines expressed her bewilderment about why her stepfather and brother had to die in war. After Jane had presented her paragraph and McKuen's poem, there was to me an unbearable silence. We all felt sympathetic about the death of two men in her family, but we didn't know what to say. Some of us didn't like Rod McKuen, but obviously she did. Nevertheless, I said, "What do you think of McKuen's poem?" One student said he thought it was pretty terrible. I said I liked the line "Some of them fall with no sound at all," but that otherwise I didn't get any feel of war in the other lines, and that the poem was so removed and nicey-nicey that the question at the end about why some soldiers die did not seem real or felt to me. Then one of the other men in class piled into McKuen's poem and demolished it. He had help from three others. Jane was naturally discomposed. But others and I added truthfully that we thought her paragraph—although confusingly phrased at times—made a stronger and more valid statement about death in war than McKuen's poem had.

☐

I went home that afternoon wondering what we literature teachers had done. Here were two seniors in college, majors in literature, who given freedom to choose poems had picked two weak, sentimental works, and apparently with admiration. But things were said against the poems by others as well as me, and we had begun the course. The reluctance of many to talk in this seminar would probably be overcome. We were on our way.

I felt better when I came upon Lorna Ridehout's work in the papers I took home with me.

### DEATH IN TWO WARS

*Wilfred Owen's poem "Greater Love" pertains to World War I, but yet I am able to relate my personal experiences with Viet Nam to his work. War is war no matter when it occurs. Reading this poem I am able to recall many memories. I have read words similar in meaning written to me. My ex-fiancé, during a twelve month tour of duty in Viet Nam, had commented many times of the love he felt for his fellow soldiers and the feelings that he experienced when they became dead heroes. "The people back home just cannot understand this feeling."*

*At the beginning I found great difficulty understanding this strong love he spoke of, but as time passed and I received pictures of his friends and stories of the crazy things that they did together, I knew them and grew fond of them. I regret that I never had the opportunity to meet them. When I heard that a death had occurred I felt emptiness and sadness, and there I was half way around the world.*

*Bob was there sharing and experiencing life with them and having one day to turn around and find them cold and lifeless lying in some trench or having their bodies splattered across a foreign land. "There we were running along, trying to make it back to the carrier, cracking jokes and talking about the idea of dying—after a while the idea of death makes you laugh. I was running ahead and that sound pierced my ears, that sound I've heard so many damn times, and just continued to run laughing. After a while I turned to see how far behind Skip was—he wasn't running any more, He was lying down. I yelled, 'Come on, kid. Charlie can't get you!' but Charlie did. He got him good. Why God? Why him? Lorna, nowadays tears come awful easy to me."*

*I know now and understand the love between soldiers.*

I was struck by this paper, I think, because upon first quick reading of Owen's poem I had missed the fact that the poet was addressing a woman as his love and contrasting his feeling for her with his love for soldiers. Lorna's paper showed me what this poem was saying. Her experience helped her read the poem; it helped me, too. Corroboration for my new course.

In class, the response to Lorna's work was almost nil. As before, no one wanted to commit himself. Lorna had put a part of her life on the table, but her classmates didn't want to talk about her paper. Sorry for her, I tried to transfer attention from her comments to Owen's poem. Losing my composure, I said, "Do you see what it is saying?" in the manner of a Test-Grade teacher. Several students said they didn't, speaking in a complaining tone against Owen, Lorna, and me. We talked and I explained, giving the Right Answer, which one of their own had already brilliantly supplied for them.

It was about this time that I sensed in that room the smell of Death. But in all my confidence I thought: just a minor illness. A little medicine . . .

☐

In this class the students appeared not to respect each other. Again and again they would not talk, refusing to comment not just on each other's work but on their own as well. Jim Born would come early to class and place in the center of the large table two Mason jars and a plastic bag full of cigarette butts and sit back and wait for reactions. I liked that, saw it was an act of art or nonart in the contemporary mode. The objects made a point to me obtruding themselves baroquely in our sterile classroom with its white walls, formica-topped table, and metal and plastic chairs. Here the butts spoke more loudly than in a museum. But when Jim brought in his work for a class assignment, I felt different. It was a prose piece he had written with no apparent connection to a literary work or film. He presented it with no prologue or afterword. I was baffled and angry, asked for responses from the class, got none, and then said to Jim:

"What did you expect us to get from that?"

"I have nothing to say. The work speaks for itself."

Yet apparently it hadn't said a word to that seminar. Goldie's admonition was becoming the model of this class.

☐

One day a student presented a collage of pictures cut from magazines. He said it spoke to the violence in war. As usual I asked the class what they felt about it. Before anyone else could respond, Bruce Bond said, "Nothing should be said by us about violence in war. The subject is beyond comment. We cannot do justice to the outrage that should be felt about it." He spoke in eloquent tones and rhythms, as if he were Moses. I thought it proper for him to refuse to comment on the work on those grounds, but not to order the others not to speak, and in a class already suffering from clamming up. I let that statement stand without countering it, expecting that some of the others in the room would discuss Bruce's position statement. No comment. It was apparently wrong not only to speak of the outrage of war but also to speak of Bruce's comments.

There were two persons in that class who steadily pursued the course described in my prospectus, Jimmy Gombara and Marilyn Muller, both of whom frequently responded to the work of others. After a few weeks Marilyn gave the class hell for not talking. I supported her, but neither of us could say what was causing the reluctance, the growing absences, the icy atmosphere.

Jan Randall and Lorna Ridehout asked me if they could invite the class to their apartment for spaghetti. They did that with beautiful hospitality and good food. When I arrived at the party with several girls I had driven there, most persons were silent, halting, or bland with each other in conversation. When I left about midnight, the talk was still not lively, except from a bubbly girl who had become a heroine because she had got slightly high on wine. Her talk was not witty or inspired bacchanal but it rose above the general stolidity. Even a party had not brought us together.

The next morning those few students who appeared in class said a number of them had stayed up drinking until 6:00 A.M. I thought maybe I had misjudged; perhaps after I left a camaraderie had developed that would raise the tone of the class. Not so. Some friendships originated, but as a whole the class continued to be uncommunicative. Marilyn, who had not attended the party, divulged that she was a young war widow by presenting a poem about giving birth to her baby. She said she had read something somewhere about motherhood—I forget what now—that had led her to compose it.

### TIME OF CHILD

*He was born once,*
*After sixteen gray, screaming hours*
*Crashing through the barrier of womb*
*Into his time.*

*Teeth-broken lips parched a smile*
*And held him, mortal's silly gift.*
*He was real to touch,*
*Made breathing, meaning life.*

*Bruised blue and black,*
*Red, sorrowful and angry,*
*An agitated cry his first sound*
*For his world.*

*He assaults her breast,*
*His first earthly meal.*
*She fights her thoughts strange.*
*"My God, I don't even know him."*

A number of persons, including me, thought the poem strong and, refreshingly, said so. Six days later one of the girls in the class—I'll call her Sue—handed me another poem and said it was in opposition to Marilyn's. She wanted it presented to the class without identification because it told of her experience giving birth to a child out of wedlock. I thought, "How good for the class to see the irony of two different perceptions of birth," but when I saw the poem I wished I had not said I would present it to the class. It was sentimental, vague, and unconvincing; and the few in the class who spoke cut it down. I tried to emphasize the validity of the impulse and the contrast. But the damage had been done to Sue. She had exposed her most intimate experience and her presentation had been rejected. Both her work and her reaction to it were purely subjective, and the class was unable to bring to it an objectivity that might have helped her. If the class had been going right, these two poems about birth would have been occasions for helpful criticism, rewriting, and a success that might have affected Sue the rest of her life.

☐

By the halfway point in the semester that Senior Seminar had become a series of painful silences and refusals by students to allow any suggestions for change in their work, or sometimes any comment at all. I tried everything I knew—gave the students a bunch of varied poems and asked them to choose one and criticize it any way they wished. About a third of the class did that assignment. I forced everyone to read one work, a portion of Thoreau's essay on wildness called "Walking," a timely statement about ecology. Little response. Most students didn't read all of it.

In a written memo I reminded the class of the prospectus for the course, which said it would balance freedom with discipline. When they didn't respond to direction, I gave them more and more freedom. This they said they liked, and they freely skipped class often and freely felt no obligation to attend to or criticize the work of their classmates.

From then on I began every class with the question "What's on your mind today?" and let the talk go. In other classes I found students in that period at their best. In Senior Seminar occasionally that opening period led to something—usually not. Frequently as I turned to the regular class activity I had the feeling there was no turn involved. The seminar presentation of work and discussion of it seemed equally disconnected and amorphous; there was no valuable opposition in the two activities.

The class became almost unbearable. I didn't want to go to it. At nights I waked thinking about it, alternately belligerent and discouraged. It was plain that my course prospectus had attracted a number of students who were on a freedom kick, who felt that letting everyone do his thing with no critical response was the highest life. And yet I knew that four of the students, whom I had taught in other classes, had earlier learned that becoming productive involves more than being free from everything and everybody. But two of those had been absent for long stretches because of sickness. The other two, who had sometimes done good work in previous classes of mine, had perhaps been then ready to retreat into total freedom but had been restrained by the example of other students.

I remember that one of those two, a girl, had presented a slide show and got more response from the group than anyone previously. Almost all of it was negative: "We didn't get that idea you mention from the pictures." She kept repeating that they should have gotten that idea from the pictures. They responded by showing how the pictures had led them elsewhere and what she might do now to redirect the viewers. But again she lectured them. "You should have got the idea." Not, apparently, because her pictures communicated that idea but because it was *her* idea. She had freely chosen it and believed in it and any suggestion that it was not palpable in that room was a reflection upon her integrity and evidence of the obtuseness of her audience.

For the last and most formidable task in the class I had assigned a slide or film project which was to echo, parallel, or comment directly or indirectly on some idea or experience in a literary or filmic work the student had been hooked by.

As a warm-up, I asked for a small visual project from everyone. I scheduled both the large and small projects, but gave leeway for things going wrong technically, etc. The performance was excruciatingly delayed and neglected by many in the class. Attendance dropped still more and those who appeared frequently did not enter the discussion of the work presented. So those who had worked hard often got no reaction and no help from learning of their mistakes or successes in their small projects, which were to be the preparing ground for the large.

I got mad, and issued an ultimatum. "Anyone who is not willing to participate in this seminar, to comment on the work of others, can drop out of class right now with a grade of B. I do not want people at this table during the presentation of final projects who hurt the class by their silence."

One student who had been among the most damaging by his unwillingness to talk either about others' work or his own, came to my office and began what I think he meant to be a bawling out. He said I had been unfair not to offer an "A" to those who might drop out. I told him that none of the silent ones—I figured six out of the fifteen in that category—had done "A" work yet. And I let him know I was disgusted with his suggestion. At that point he broke down and admitted that he had not contributed much because in all his classes he was too frightened to speak more than a few times in the whole semester. I later found he was a sophomore who had sneaked into this senior class through shenanigans involving nepotism. That was a crushing interview for both of us. I knew that if I had started off students at their strength that boy might have turned a big corner in his life.

☐

Four students dropped out and took "B's." One was Ben Whorl, who had never opened up again after that first day when he showed us the slide of the plane in the sunset. Another was a fairly productive boy who had recently instituted a poetry supplement to the campus newspaper in which several poems from our seminar appeared. I was sorry to lose him, but thought my action proper. I still do, although it is not an act I remember proudly. Like all my other strategems in that class it did little to improve performance.

The ridiculous limits to which this group of bright young persons went—supposedly under my tutelage but seldom taking direction from me or each other—is illustrated by the response the leader of the freedom forces, Bruce Bond, received from his comrades. He had been working with friends to get money to establish a Free School in town for high-school-age students. He wanted to bring in the first draft of their prospectus and get the seminar's response. Once again, I was getting into the situation I believe a good course produces—where a student honors the university by expecting it to help him with what counts for him and what may count for the larger community.

I read the prospectus and felt the same chill I had experienced when Sue brought in her poem about giving birth to a child. The motive was healthy, the communication poor. Bruce's pretentious statement pursued the false belief that freedom would automatically create good works. After Bruce had grandly invited the class to read the document and help him and I had supported his request, he passed out dittoed copies.

At the next meeting Bruce was absent, typically. When he appeared at the following class, no apologies, but much expectation of what the others would say about his document. Most had forgotten it entirely. One had read it. Out of all those freedom lovers only one had taken the trouble to read a description of a Free School written by the spokesman for untrammeled freedom. I distributed copies of the document to those who had missed the previous class or lost the work. Two weeks after the invitation only three students had read it. We had a short and unsatisfactory discussion, I doing most of the talking.

☐

That seminar was a failure, and the major cause of it was the teacher, who did not set up the course so the students became productive. At the end of the semester the students and I trusted less in each other than at the beginning, and students had dropped away from each other instead of coming together like persons who see they are helping and teaching each other.

I have not cited all the valuable papers and film and slide shows that were done in that class, but they were no more than occasional surprises compared to those that appeared in the Shakespeare and Advanced Writing courses I was teaching at the same time in the same university. As a result of seminar criticism, what was good was seldom made better and what was mediocre was seldom made good. In the Shakespeare course I had frequently taped class discussions and published them in a book or played them at teachers' conferences. The responses were consistently appreciative. I would have been chagrined to have played a tape of almost any day's meeting of Senior Seminar.

My first failure was in not arranging for the students to do something at their strength. Once a number of them began presenting weak works to each other, their confidence was undermined, not only in themselves, but in the ability of the other students and me to comment on work presented there. So much depends. About four weeks into the semester I realized the seriousness of my error. I could not then save the course. I had promised these students a new life—not a new kind of test or reading list but performance from them that would delight them and others. Early on they could see they were missing more often than hitting.

If I had begun the course properly, it would not have gone well because so much also depends on establishing a discipline of continuity. In the Shakespeare course the students were free to initiate their statements in class about a character or play we had read. And free to choose what character in a play they would write about, or later, to write on any aspect of the plays they had read, and still later, to bring any part of their experience up against any part of a play. But the range had some limitation. We read (I mean *we*) nine Shakespeare plays. I chose them. There was no doubt that at any time at least thirty of the thirty-eight students had read the play that was being discussed in class or in a paper read aloud. All that variety of perception, based on all that variety of personal experience behind each reading and comment. Those differences were balanced, and sometimes polarized, by what they had in common, a close reading and rereading of one work by one author printed in one edition which each student owned. The text was unchangeable, absolutely there. In that class—something in common, and a great deal in difference. We could talk to each other and wanted to. In the Senior Seminar we had the fat of freedom without the bones of communication, habit, continuity.

This is one of the few valid purposes for establishing schools and bringing persons together in groups at appointed, regular times: to play the perceptions of many against each other as they consider one work, one set of facts, one theory, or one view of the natural or human world. What is considered may come from the students or the teacher.

In a proper school the persons in a class are peers. One respects his peers because he can talk best to them and understand them. The teacher is older; his age plays against their youth and creates a tension. They see what this woman or man does not see; she sees what they do not see. Her calm, maturity, or nervousness is different from their calm, maturity, and nervousness. In some ways they are more mature than she. If she makes herself another person in the class and still remains a leader who induces the others to follow her directions as well as theirs, she becomes an Enabler. So much depends on experiencing polarities— freedom and discipline, commonality and individualism, subjectivity and objectivity.

Chapter 5

# A Thoreau Course

□

The tendency to magnify the moment, to read all the laws of Nature in the one object or one combination under your eye, is of course comic to those who do not share the philosopher's perception of identity. To him [Thoreau] there was no such thing as size.

Ralph Waldo Emerson, "Thoreau"

□

For thirty-five years Henry Thoreau has had me hooked on the end of his line. For ten I have lived on a pond in the same latitude as Walden. I once vowed that when I was rich enough I would buy the fourteen-volume edition of his journals. Before that time I hungered so for them that I bought the two-volume Dover edition in which four pages of the original plates are printed on one large page. For a year I read in that vast Concord of Thoreau's mind, and decided it was time to launch a course in him.

English 555, The Art and Thought of Thoreau, 4–5:40 P.M. In the written announcement I said that students would keep journals in order to see better the central act of Thoreau's writing life. Out of his journals he built his books and essays and lectures.

In writing of this class, I'll use pseudonyms for everyone because I'm too close to risk names. The group was so small I fear the students will always recognize those I mention. I liked and respected every student. I hope everyone in the class senses that I am being candid here in order to report what I see as the truth of that experience, not to praise or condemn individuals. Eight undergraduates and five graduates. And one auditor, a young mother in another of my classes who said she loved Thoreau and wanted to sit in. I started to say no, but she was so sweet and sincere that I relented. I have never taught a class in which auditors did not drop out halfway through the semester or earlier.

□

On the first day I gave my usual talk about honesty—this time laced with examples of Thoreau's discipline in making his words carry their weight—and asked for two free writings in class. The free writings were neither better nor worse than usual. Every student had written a few lines which seemed to merit our attention. I typed them, dittoed them, as usual, and brought them to the table. Sid took us immediately into one of Henry's major subjects—the meaning in work:

> I've been here since Sunday but until last night I felt so totally out of it. All summer at work I thought this job's only temporary—you can cope, but yet I couldn't imagine actually being back on campus. Maybe I quit work too late—the past Friday. I'm still in the assembly line rut—48 cars an hour, 48 steering wheel columns an hour. In fact, I start work in 7 minutes—5:30. . . .

The other free writings corroborated my belief that the design of this course was simple and right; I had no difficulty describing it. I asked the students to write journals like Thoreau's: records of events and thoughts that came from where they were. Their Concord might be the grease pit of a gas station or the drab halls of a dormitory. Thoreau might have the advantage that he was writing out of love, but they would necessarily have to tell what flowered out of their ground, or discovered itself in an oil puddle. They could not be like Thoreau unless they were themselves. I asked them also to write in their journals their responses to reading Thoreau, and we began with Carl Bode's *Selected Journals of Thoreau* (1967). I told the students they would find how easy and hard it was to do what Thoreau had done. They would find themselves unwittingly working out of their experience toward his conclusions. They would discover what he was saying because of what they said. Their experience would tell them he was wrong and he was right. I found myself saying again and again that they would *find* this or *discover* that. I was right. It proved to be a finding course.

Within the week Sid found our man in a park and recorded the meeting:

*It was 11:30 p.m. I had just finished reading 600 pages of* The Brothers Karamazov *and even though I took my time—3 hours—I was quite fatigued and tensed up. So I drank half my capacity as far as beer goes—one can—and decided to take a walk. I live near a small park, one which I've never walked through, so I decided to do some exploring.*

*I noticed something stirring on one of the green park benches. As I began to circle around towards home, this stirring figure became identifiable: a young looking white dude, moderate length black hair, carrying a sleeping bag. He came up to me and asked if I had a cigarette. I replied negatively and asked him the question I had heard so much of when I was hitchhiking around the country: Where you coming from and where are you headed? Tim—that was his name—was from San Pedro, California, but he was born here. He had moved out to Cal with his parents when he was 14 but they came back after only a year. He didn't. He stayed with his uncle for a year or so and then struck out on his own. Although one couldn't tell from looking at him—he looked almost straight, as opposed to being a "head"—he had lived in San Francisco during the Haight-Ashbury district's golden years, 1966 and 1967. He was one of the original flower children. And what established his hippie precocity even more (to me, anyway) was the fact that way back in 1965 he got busted in Disneyland for smoking that dread and infamous weed—marijuana. . . .*

*I told him a little about myself, how I had hitchhiked to Cal last summer and how life on the road appealed to me. Tim said that he had no special reason for leaving Cal. He had just got the urge, so he left, even though he was moderately in love with a 20-year-old "Christian," a girl who attended church 6 or 7 days a week. She didn't like sin, Tim said. He told me that at 23 he was*

*still searching for that nebulous something but was happy. He
considered himself a "rich person" even though he owned only
his sleeping bag and a few clothes. People get trapped, he commented; they start becoming more and more greedy or spoiled so
that they can't live without their needless luxuries. Tim had one
good job in San Pedro. He was a manager of a men's clothing
department, making good money and practically doing nothing.
One day he was leaning against the counter, bored, when some of
his friends came in and meanly told him they were going surfing,
too bad he couldn't go. Well, Tim wondered what exactly he was
doing inside a clothing store on such a nice day. So he quit the
job on the spot—never to return—and went surfing. "I like truck-
in," Tim said. "If I want to go somewhere or do something, I do it."*

*Since I'm reading* Walden *for one class and Thoreau's journals
for this one, Thoreau was on my mind. I asked Tim if he had ever
heard of Henry David Thoreau. He hadn't. So briefly I recounted
Thoreau's life, emphasizing Henry's obsession with simplicity. I
mentioned some of Thoreau's famous statements; one was the one
about how men "lead lives of quiet desperation," or as Tim said,
"get trapped." Another statement concerned the same "getting
trapped" motif, or as Thoreau put it, "Men have become the tools
of their tools." The last statement " . . . the cost of a thing is the
amount of what I will call life which is required to be exchanged
for it, immediately or in the long run"—impressed Tim to the
point of noticeable excitement. . . .*

Sally recorded a nature walk with a man who knew the woods
well. She clarified her narrative with pen drawings of leaves and plants
(some in small section) they had observed. That is what Thoreau did
in his journals. I did not tell her to do that.

Yolanda, the young mother who was auditing, recorded like Thoreau an encounter with an animal. She told of hitting a cat while driving, and then let herself slip away into other memories, again like Thoreau:

> *. . . My aunt died and she rotted in her one-room apartment for
> four days before she was found. The mortician said she was
> bloated and green. She had hemorrhaged and my mother said
> there was an outline of her body on the floor. She was forty and
> died of a heart attack. It's been nearly two years and I still won't
> think about it for long, even though I sometimes think I want to.*

The students began to see how a journal writer rambles and why
his meanderings of the mind are often exciting and sometimes exasper-
ating. Sam wrote about raking leaves, and slipped off into carving fascinating cameos of a neighbor and his father:

I raked leaves for a man of letters who lived on the edge of Sherwood Forest, an Eskimo who was handed a snow shovel during the light season and told to work till dark. Only one consolation—no dog—hence no hidden piles of dog shit.

A retired professor called and offered me a leaf raking job. Since a can of green peas in the cupboard ain't much security, I accepted. The entire operation consumed seven hours, for which I was reimbursed eighteen dollars—both of which are now gone.

The leaves, mostly oak, were one to two feet deep over lawns, drives, patios, vines, rock gardens, and gravel beds. I had to load them into a barrel which weighed about seventy-five pounds when full, and drag it over a narrow path winding about two hundred yards into the woods to dump it. The path was a foot wide and muddy, strewn with rocks, brambles, and branches. Oh yes, it rained all the while too.

I quit, to myself, about eight times before I finished. Between the times I quit, my mind would occupy itself while the body machine toiled. I hated those leaves. Rocco loved them. Rocco was a retired city sewer digger, off the boat, who lived across the street from our house. He grew a garlic garden. Every fall he would make a formal, humble request for our leaf piles to bed down his garlics. He'd carefully collect all the leaves into bushels and carry them home. He raised pigeons for fertilizing purposes too. Rocco was so happy that he'd return with a gallon of dago red. He died last fall—the garlic garden did too. Someone should cover over his plot with leaves. I think he'd like that.

A leaf caught on the end of a tine and vibrated like wings of a captured bird—so much so that I snapped out of the trance in a panic to see if it actually was a bird.... no, just a leaf.

My boss was inside reading—probably poems—he was the type. "Well, I know how to read some poems too," I thought,

> The trees are in their autumn beauty
> The woodland paths are dry ...

That didn't work.

The leaf pile was ten feet high—cone-shaped with the base having a radius of fifteen feet. This was work—I mean scientifically it was work—moving an object (or objects) with force a certain distance. It still didn't make sense. It reminds me of my father in the summer.

He would take down the small flat-bottom boat from garage rafters and rest it on top of two sawhorses. Then he'd collect all the cushions, lights, ropes and anchor, oars and fishing tackle and place them inside. He'd hang the small motor over the back end in a waterfilled oil drum and run it till all the beer was gone. By then it's too late to go anywhere but at least there was always next Saturday. Last year he bought a bigger boat, which sits

*moored to a dock. He runs that and can drink inside of it too.*
*Damn leaves.*

We discussed how Thoreau brought persons into his journals that primarily recorded the natural world he walked through in his afternoons. We decided that he also contented himself with vignettes of people. We found no extended portrait in the journals. The best that I remember is his journal entry of October 4, 1851, on George Minott.

☐

In journals the students quickly forgot their classroom selves and found themselves elsewhere. As I suspected, they let Henry influence them—bring a subject into their ken—and then lit out on their own from there, or moved back into their past from that point.

*So, it is October already—the turning, churning of the days like*
*in those old movies when to indicate the passage of time they*
*flick the pages of a calendar rapidly so that the numbers almost*
*run together.*
*At what point in a person's life does he no longer want to see*
*the new day and what it has to offer him? At what age does a*
*person want life to stand still; when does he want to live over and*
*over that one tender day for the rest of his life?*
*I cannot remember a time when I didn't look forward to the*
*new day. At the end of a vacation I'm ready to get home—altho*
*never before its end. Even when there was something I dreaded I*
*didn't want to prolong the leap. There was almost an excitement,*
*some sort of masochistic pleasure in getting the "unpleasantness"*
*behind me. How dull it would be to live the "perfect day" over*
*and over until you knew every move in a kind of slow-motion*
*dream, heard every beautiful word droned on so that you knew*
*every inflection, every nuance by heart.*

When I read this passage by Patti aloud, one student said, "I don't believe it. You mean you *always* looked forward to the new day?"

"Yes," said Patti, and we talked about Thoreau's similar astounding optimism, his never subsiding morning cheerfulness. Both Patti and Henry were accused of romanticizing by those sitting around our table.

☐

Frequently students brought to class a contemporary mention of Thoreau. And soon articles and stories and poems were being presented by students who—like teachers—could not refrain from sharing a correspondence they had noticed between the man we were studying and someone in their world today.

Rod read aloud a long article from *Time* about the new ritualism in America. Thoreau had not written about that subject in anything we had agreed to read, but the article went at ritualism in a way that would have excited Thoreau, and I thought of how fine of Rod to risk taking our time for that article. I can remember years ago in conventional classes being bored by a student who tried to impress Teacher by "bringing something in." Usually it was both irrelevant and empty. But here the article brought in was loaded with Thoreau's concerns. It moved out from, maybe paralleled Henry's thought, and stretched us to think further—the way all teachers would like their students to act.

Several students began copying down short passages from other writers in their journals. They were doing precisely what Thoreau, Emerson, and many other writers customarily did—keeping a commonplace book, a personal anthology of writings they cared for. Sam put this passage down and I dittoed it for class:

> *Speakin' o' the scenery, it certainly was somethin' grand. First we'd pass a few pine trees with fuzz on 'em (Spanish moss) and then a couple o' acres o' yellow mud. Then they'd be more pine trees and more fuzz and then more yellow mud. And after a w'ile we'd come to some pine trees with fuzz on 'em and then, if we watched close, we'd see some yellow mud.*

> *Gullible's Travels*

I had spoken to Sam in class about cutting some of his wasted words in journal entries. Perhaps he was thinking of that when he wrote down Ring Lardner's passage. Whatever, it was useful to us, both as instruction in what to avoid in our own writing, and as contrast to the usually succinct nature descriptions of Thoreau.

□

In the third week, to break from Thoreau's journals, I asked students to read his essay, "Civil Disobedience." In her journal Patti said that the day Thoreau spent in jail to protest taxes imposed by a government pursuing a war against Mexico was not proof enough for her that he practiced what he preached. A long term, or a lifetime, in jail, she said, would speak differently.

Diane reported that she married a man who had not paid his last three years' income tax because of the Vietnam War. She told him, "Let's pay, because now I'm part of your life and I don't want to take responsibility for your principles." She said she was beginning to accept the truth of her husband's charge that she was forever trying to be conventional. In almost all the discussions we had of this kind, I sensed the students were not simply trying—as I had in college—to find something in their life that might please the teacher by its relation to the writing we were studying, but rather were facing the same or similar problems as those Thoreau faced, and in earnest.

Already in the first weeks of the class the students' experience and Thoreau's were becoming entangled like two strands of hemp. Together they were beginning to form a strong rope. Will wrote:

> *I really liked HDT's description of a marine: "a mere shadow and reminiscence of humanity, a man laid out alive and standing, and already, as one might say, buried under arms with funeral accompaniments. . . ."*

And Marvin wrote:

> *I played some war games at Ft. Custer this weekend with the Army Reserves. Saturday night I was killed by the enemy. Since I was dead I decided to celebrate by drinking the beer I had smuggled into camp. The unit commander caught me and was a little upset. I explained to him that I was dead, why should I not drink? He became more upset. As punishment he resurrected me from the grave, giving me life, and made me pull guard duty all night. Even in death there is a unit commander.*

☐

In this seminar I managed a refreshing balance between my students' experience and the experience in the books we were reading. We spent half of the hour-and-fifty-minute period reading Thoreau. I assigned perhaps thirty pages in his journals. When we were seated around the table, I asked, "Anyone have anything to say about the first page? Anything strike you hard? Remind you of something in your experience? Seem wrong or unusually right?" And then a fine discussion would begin. From time to time I commented on passages that I had checked in my book. We asked no grilling questions of each other. It was not a game to see who knew the most, but an exchange of responses. Occasionally we explored a difference of opinion. Because there were no confining, cabining questions from the chair, the students often talked brilliantly, bringing long-held thoughts and remembered experience to bear upon the development of an opinion.

Then for the rest of the period I read excerpts from the students' journals, which I had typed and dittoed and distributed. They recorded not only parallel or contrasting experience to Thoreau's, but also their reactions to reading him.

In the second week Diane wrote:

> *Thoreau's entries often leave me hanging as if the personal experiences are not to be fully shared by me. Lots of incongruities (i.e. "We make our own fortune" p. 28). What does an unsink-*

*able cork (man) have to do with viewing the world through a "chink or knothole"?*

I had said that I thought the purpose of coming together to study any writer must be for us to help each other read him better. Diane admitted her difficulties, and the class helped her understand the passages that puzzled her. Later in the year we were often to find some of Henry's passages finally—and sometimes unfortunately—ambiguous or misleading.

☐

If the seminar had been extended to two semesters—as some students wished—I believe it would have carried the possibility of our learning everything about reading and writing. There was not time to reorganize, sharpen, or polish our writing. Overall the writing in this class did not match in quality that done in classes devoted to writing. We had to spend more than half our time on Thoreau's words. In that task I think we excelled. We debated almost every major point about Thoreau that I think has been discussed by scholars, but the observations arose from those of us seated around that table. Sid said Henry beatified nature dangerously. Will said he was too quick to call other men jackasses. We discussed Thoreau's lack of sexual relationships with women. His strained friendship with Emerson. His traveling. His politics. His attitude toward Indians. I did not bring up these topics, merely joined the debate.

In dozens of ways in that seminar we were doing natural and useful things in reading and writing for ourselves and each other. That I am so impressed with our behavior may surprise a reader no longer immersed in school. He might think, "Why not? Is there a radically different way from this commonsense approach?" Yes there is. It is the traditional school way, which controls one's hands and brains, one's tongue and emotions. It wipes out one's past, and plots his present in little numbered squares to be filled in with a paint brush.

In this class we all corrected each other's reading, not with red pencil, not by giving test scores, but simply by helping each other. I have never before seen so little animosity and contentiousness in a seminar. As we explored Thoreau's life and ours in journals we found him often narrower than us, and usually deeper. Patti wrote:

> *My son, my middle child, the handsome one, the worst student, the one most admired by his peers, came home from football practice tonight sick, with a belly-ache, half-crying.*
> *Thirteen years old, short for his age—but tough—he pedals off on his bike at 5:00 p.m. and drags back into the house around 8:00 every night after smashing into his friends' bodies, grappling with thundering legs, and suffering the humiliations of the shout-*

ing coach ("Kill 'em") so that he can become a "man" in this upside-down world of ours.

A half-cold dinner waits for him in the kitchen. I rush him out there so that he can eat, shower, and riffle through the pages of his homework before he groans into bed. "Sound mind, healthy body," I tell myself. Also, he was turning to fat this summer and the physical exercise is good for him. And I don't forget to remind myself that if most of his friends are playing football and he isn't, then there is no one to occupy his time, nothing for him to do between school and bedtime.

But tonight is different. He eats little, is too sick. I tell him that it was the peanut butter sandwich he ate before practice. I tell him that big Scott M. across the street throws up after every practice if he eats less than two hours before. Reed trudges upstairs to suffer alone.

After his shower he goes to his room, where he thinks no one can hear him. But I hear him; he is crying. I try not to worry, for he is the one who moans even when he has a minor cold. It is hard for him to adjust to these unknown physical affronts to his body. Too, also briefly, I think of those other times when he has cried because something which he couldn't cope with was gnawing at him. I will wait a while, see what develops.

When he comes downstairs, I ask him if the practice went badly, if the coach was after him. No—he just feels sick. I tell him that he cannot watch television, that he needs to lie down in his room. The others come. The impatient one who is playing clarinet and never learned the names of the notes. Now she is in trouble because the band is playing in B-flats and G-flats. We draw pictures of the scale with the letters in the spaces and lines. The brilliant one, almost a woman, wanders in and out, thinking of clothes and talking about being an exchange student. I hear Reed in the distance, still crying behind closed doors.

At last he appears. I put down my book. He sits at the foot of my bed, still young enough to weep, and tries to talk. The others hover, then vanish. They know this is his crisis.

"Lorie is going to leave soon," he finally manages to blubber out. But I tell him—No, that she won't be going to college for years yet.

"I don't want anything to change."

The crack begins to open just a little. "Do you want to stay just like you are?" I ask. Of course he does, and nods, and then it all comes spilling, tumbling out, a waterfall of worry and sadness and tears. As he tells it, I remember how, when he was ten, he worried about what would become of us when the sun burned out—how, when he was nine, he worried about having to fight in Vietnam. This tough boy-child, whom we worry about with his D's and C's, has more depth to him than any of our others.

*What will happen to him if his father dies? If I die? What will he do if he lives to be 103 and there is no family left? How will he stand it when they put him in a box in the ground? Was he born to learn to walk and talk and do a few things and then just die? Why can't everything just stay as it is, instead of being over with so fast?*

*My God, I wonder, did the philosophers think of these things when they were young boys after their soccer games in the park? Did I ever think of them when I was a girl and tired of rocking dolls? Can it be that we have always thought these things, somewhere deep in the blackness of ourselves?*

*We laugh that when he is 103, Annie may be 104, and Lorie 105. I tell him that when he goes away to college, I will expect him to come back now and then. We talk about change, how people make plans to do things in the future, how I will miss him but won't be lonely. And we think about his new family that he will have when he leaves his old family.*

*I remember that he wants to live on an Indian reservation and help the Indians (He knows every tribe and every chief. They are the only books he reads). We talk about planning to do something worthwhile in this life, of preparing ourselves to help others, how this will make our short life meaningful (I remember the D's and C's).*

*But most of all, we talk about the wooden box. I ask him if he knows that the Indians believe that their spirits will always walk on the Earth, that the Earth is their mother. Of course he knows. Had I forgotten that he knows everything about the Indian? I tell him that our bodies do die, wear out like old cars, but that our minds stay alive like the Indian Spirits. They float out of the box—right away (This is important, I think)—and walk on the Earth, or float to a new planet maybe, or change into another body. Yes, they are happy. Yes, if your spirit saw people on the street, it would laugh to see them. I tell him that the body doesn't care. The body is like an old coat and I wouldn't care if I shrugged off my old coat and left it in a box somewhere, would he?*

*"But if you don't want to leave this life?"*

*Did he want to leave the life he was in before he was born? I ask. We don't know what it was like before. But he knows that he is happy with this life. I tell him that the other life was probably worse than this one, so that his next one will probably be better still. Each life gets better. It must. And you must then take something of the old life with you into the new one for a memory. What did he think he had brought with him from the old life before he was born?*

*Have I done a good job? I don't know. He is not crying any more. He tells me that he has been worrying about this for a week and hasn't been able to eat much. We laugh and both agree that the not-eating was probably good for him.*

*It is much later now. He is sleeping. Everyone is sleeping. I hope his spirit sleeps well.*

*    *    *

*Henry Thoreau was not married; he had no children. His intimacies were with nature and he only wrote about people in a generalized way. Thoreau knew Death, however. He had watched his brother die, but preferred not to write about it. His own impending death was apparent to him, yet even then, he chose to speak about a living world.*

*I am married, have children. I'm sorry for Henry; I think he missed a big part of life. My intimacies are with people I love. Nature is secondary for me; I prefer to share myself with people and to write about the meaningful moments that enter my life through human encounters, even if that means that I must write about death. Walk in peace, Henry.*

Patti wrote that passage out of one of her many strengths. It was possible in this simply designed class to lead from one's strength. Will was a history major and could use his knowledge to help us see why Henry was so hard on the politicians of his day:

*How could that well-educated man from Cambridge, Mass., dislike the politicians of his time with equal intensity as the railroad? The men who took it upon themselves (or did they stumble onto it?) to lead this country during its bubbling Nationalistic period (later interpreted as feeling its oats) were people of such great stature with resumés and credentials that make people stand in awe: A. Jackson (Old Hickory), his famous acts include the fighting of a battle that didn't need to be fought (let alone with help of a French pirate wanted for murder, rape, and other less auspicious acts), and overseeing the crudest, most barbaric, drunken affair ever held at the White House, namely his inaugural. Henry Clay, the Great Compromiser (meaning he didn't have a single thought of his own—he just took two opposing viewpoints, put them together and signed his name). Mr. Tyler, the poorer half of a comedy team with an insatiable thirst for Russian vodka. One J. Polk, whose claim to fame was the installation of central heating in the White House after one of his mistresses complained vigorously one December evening, coupled with the invasion of a third-rate country. Said M. Fillmore, whose famous deeds include the abortive attempt to establish an all-water route from New York to California and the changing of our national symbol from the eagle to the turkey. The list of acts is endless from these gentlemen. Come to think of it, while the railroads were tearing up the countryside, the politicians were tearing up the country.*

What a rare occurrence in American universities—a student majoring in one field bringing his special knowledge to students and teacher in another!

☐

Not every student was working at full strength. Vicki wrote two pages in her journal while the others were writing ten to thirty. Short passages, like this entry:

*Traffic is heavy. Up ahead are two lanes of ants leaving a picnic. It's sure nice to be home. The ants are smaller and not so noisy. The country is beautiful. Why do people live in cities?*

Like Thoreau she could write a good metaphor. Her entry spoke to one of Henry's subjects: the country vs. the city. I talked to her after class. "Write more." Her response suggested that would be difficult for her.

Marvin was also sparing in journal entries. Among his few pages I found this comment that sounded like Henry writing in 1972:

*I wonder if the CBS eye is looking back? I hope not. It would see too much. People say they don't like to watch the news because it's always bad. All the bad news is in the home.*

Yolanda, the auditor, dropped out. I vowed I would never again let a person audit a seminar. Two other girls were not doing enough work. Nora and Sally seldom joined in to help others see how they were writing or reading. I had spoken to both after class—as I had to Vicki—and they said they would try harder, but I was not sure they could break the fear that traditional education or other experience unknown to me had produced.

Both frequently wrote in their journals their doubts about themselves. I hate that, for I know that one begins communicating with others powerfully not by telling them his troubles but by going from himself out into the observation of others, by showing things and people in action in an objective enough way that others can see them alive. In doing so, the writer tells about himself without appearing to. Then comes communication and understanding and admiration and work and more success. So I was disturbed as I read the first paragraph of Nora's journal entry on November 8:

*i'm afraid to turn this journal in. there are so few entries in it i expect to walk into class the next time and sit down next to*

*ken - only to have him turn on me, growling and spitting out,
"why the hell aren't you writing in your journal - you haven't
read much about Thoreau or at least you haven't told us if you
have!" and then sit and glare at me while i stumble for an excuse.*

But the remaining paragraphs in that entry showed me that Nora had
at last broken through, pulled the stopper and let the words come out:

*actually i was going to start this entry talking about time - that is
trying to organize mine. last night i sat down and made a bunch
of lists - things to accomplish in a week - things i would like to
learn or do over a month - vague lifetime goals on another list. i
intended to cross off many of those items and for the first week i
did but then the second week, we had unexpected company for
three days - the following week i had lapsed back into my old
patterns of coming home from work - throwing a dinner together,
dishes, reading a magazine and or washing hair, clothes. i try to
read Thoreau but many times i find his notes send me daydream-
ing about our farm up north. i haven't been up there since last
spring. actually it no longer is "our" farm, as my uncle bought it
from his brothers and sisters, about a year ago. It was my grandfather's. A big beautiful cobblestone house he built by hand in
1918. And two huge barns (a friend, who is a builder—says he
has yet to figure out how they put the roof on—"it's self-
supporting," he says—"three stories high"). At one time there
were over seven hundred acres of land—including a lake, that was
all ours except for its northern boundary.*

*My grandfather raised white-face cattle. My recollections of
him are always times when he was with those animals. He would
stand on top of a hill that overlooked the lake and start calling to
cattle that many times i couldn't even see - "Hey billy, hey billy"
- they'd start coming out from behind bushes and climb this high
hill to get some grain or oats out of his pail.*

*The farm included about 100 acres of woods - there was a
tractor trail winding through it way back to an old unused wheat
field - we used to walk down the path in the fall collecting huge
bouquets of crimson leaves - a stream that ran through the woods
got plugged up before it reached the lake - forming a spooky
cedar swamp. At least it seemed that way in the early summer -
in autumn it was bright with bittersweet.*

*In 1962-63 a real estate man approached the family about
"developing" the lake. My grandparents had been dead many
years and my mom's brothers and sister (5 altogether) were
starting to dicker over what to do with the lake and the farmhouse and barns. The farmhouse was only used during the
summer as a vacation cottage and in the fall for deer hunting.
[This is not finished!]*

Nora had finally said two things that we all knew would interest Thoreau: her grandfather had a magic way of calling animals, and some fools were cutting into pieces a great tract of the earth. We knew what Henry would say about both things. As I wrote that comment I realized this should be one of the tests in a literature course: can the readers think like the writer they are studying? If not, they know him only partially.

Nora's way of writing—lower-case *i* and spaced hyphens replacing most punctuation marks—incensed me. When I typed ditto masters from her journal, I was constantly having to correct my mistakes and hers. I sometimes couldn't tell the relation of groups of her words because they were strung together—or was it separated?—by those damned hyphens. But since I have found that students begin writing well when they can forget punctuation and grammar and write fast and freely, I have been loath to speak to eccentric writers like her. I wanted to tell her that those professionals who have made up their own system of punctuation and capitalization—don marquis and e. e. cummings, for example—did so with great consistency. I was going to tell her and the class that the intelligent writer learns to follow the rules and see where they get him before he devises new ones. So I went to my volume of the collected works of e. e. cummings to type out a few samples for her. To my amazement I found that he was not consistent. In a number of poems he used capital letters to start sentences early and late in a work, and in between slipped back into uncapitalized style. So I gave up that idea and suffered reading the Nora System. (But I do not admire Nora or e. e. for their inconsistencies.)

Sally was also hung up in that self-examination stage.

> *The better part of man is soon plowed into the soil for compost. By a seeming fate commonly called necessity, they are employed, as it says in the good book, laying up treasures which moth and rust will corrupt and thieves break through and steal.... HDT*
>
> *I feel as if I were plowing my better part "into the soil for compost." I am not performing vibrantly. I put hours into a big bubble-gum machine and lose my money. I furiously bang on the machine to lose even more time by this useless physical exertion.*
>
> *The frustration has no outlet. I cannot conquer the loss with this anger. The function of the machine is also to ignore my protests. It only responds to more pennies.*
>
> *How can I fit myself into an atmosphere that is so conducive to my growth that all my human potential is required? What is my potential is my first question. Can you sell a fondness for older people? Is a knowledge of good fishing spots in the supply and demand balance? I probably wouldn't care if I were plowing my "better part" into a soil if that soil was of my own choosing....*

But Sally began talking a little more in class and said she felt some-what loosened up. Her journal continued spasmodically. A little work occasionally, then a spurt, then nothing. She has a beautifully original way of seeing the world, and is on the edge of showing it fully to others. I wish she had begun to do sustained work in the way Nora did. Maybe she will soon. I know that the members of that seminar know her capabilities and wish her the will to be more productive.

In my own journal writing I was not keeping up with the most prolific writers. I told myself that the exhausting hours I spent typing student work on dittoes for all my classes kept me from more journal writing. But I suspect that others in the class who were doing less, or only as much as I, had their excuses also.

Will, the history student, was running a business in another town while attending school. A rare resource in that class—a businessman who respected Thoreau but was no romantic. He missed a great many classes, never saw that he was hurting the seminar by his absences. Near the end of the course he missed meetings at which I intended—with the help of the others—to make him aware when he was overwriting or being unclear. He could say things strongly, but was highly inconsistent. There was no chance to begin this final examination of his work and develop the criticism slowly enough so he could take it.

☐

Others in the class were powering along. Sid, Diane, and Patti were writing so many long and well-focused entries into their journals that I began to feel ambivalent toward those volumes they laid on the table for me. I knew I would enjoy reading them but they took so much time along with my other school work that on many nights I found myself without opportunity for reading anything of my own choosing.

At the end of each class I would say, "Anyone who has a journal for me, please hand it in." I had asked students to buy two volumes, so they could be writing in one while I was reading the other. I never set a date for handing in journals; most students turned one in every week or ten days. At every class meeting but one I was given enough journal writing to enable me to extract enough valuable passages for publication of several pages in a dittoed handout for the next meeting. I could never predict exactly what I was going to get, but soon I began to expect some comments from Nora and Diane about holding down an unchallenging job, from Patti about living with a husband and children, from Sam about being Irish, from Will about running a business. There was variety for me and for those who listened to the entries I brought to class.

Diane filled dozens and dozens of pages in her journal with entries that spoke to Thoreau directly and indirectly. Occasionally she allowed herself to feel sorry for herself—as Thoreau seldom did.

*Nothing interests me lately. I don't ask why because that is a dead end question. All I want to do is start feeling good again. Poof! I guess I'm willing to work at feeling good but what do I do? I could go to a bar and get lit, or quit school or my job and take off. Somehow, though, the extreme isn't right for me now. I'm still hung up on responsibility. But I don't want to talk about responsibility. I know enough about that.*

*A therapist might say to start looking at what is obvious. And a writer might say: give details. But I want somebody to give me something—anything.*

I took a book to class that day (Dickens' *Bleak House*), read Diane's entry, and then handed her the book. "Someone has given you something," I said. She has been in three of my classes, and such a positive force in all of them that I felt almost like giving her my whole library.

☐

I began myself to feel the pressure of Thoreau's and my students' honesty. That meant I should write when I felt a thought weighing upon me. One day I typed out a two-page entry. I have here omitted the first fourth of it, which is talky and unnecessary. I am reminded that my students never get such a late third chance to edit their work.

*Henry Thoreau says on page 382 of* Walden *(Viking Portable, 1964):*

> *while I enjoy the friendship of the seasons I trust that nothing can make life a burden to me.*

*and goes on in one of those headlong rushes of association until he is pleased with a rainy, supposedly drear, day and praising seeds rotting in the ground and potatoes destroyed in the lowlands. It will make good grass on the uplands, and "being good for the grass, it would be good for me." In every capillary of his body he was always the ecologist.*

*Later he says:*

> *I have never felt lonesome, or in the least oppressed by a sense of solitude, but once, and that was a few weeks after I came to the woods, when, for an hour, I doubted if the near neighborhood of man was not essential to serene and healthy life.*

*On the next page he tells of becoming so sensitized to pine needles and the atmosphere, that he thought "no place could ever be strange to me again."*

*So there Henry is in the woods feeling the expansion of the pine needle and he is not lonely. I used to think that paeans to nature were sentimental and romantic. When I was separated from my first wife and nearing divorce, I rented a 70-acre wood and pasture land in the country and lived there alone, except for my young Labrador Retriever. At first the loneliness was destructive. I brought home a pint of chocolate ice cream and ate the whole package while watching television shows I didn't like. I got in my car and drove away to see bad movies. After a few months I began to relax and started to walk the woods.*

*Along the edge of a great tamarack swamp I found the blue gentian and in spring clumps of waxy marsh marigolds that pushed up before the more domesticated flowers bloomed, blazing yellow in the brown-grey lifeless landscape. Every time I went out I made discoveries. My hills later blushed blue and purple with lupine. And box turtles, and the sound of the woodcock, and puffing foolish adders, and on and on, never a walk without stunning surprises. I listened, I smelled, I saw. And gradually the pain and loneliness leaked out of me at all joints, at the seams of my eyes, running down the bones of my ears.*

*Later, when I was divorced I met a woman I cared for who was living away from her husband and considering divorce. She and I thought we might someday marry. But she decided she had to keep her family intact and went back to her husband. Once again the loneliness dropped on me and I was back to pints of ice cream and rantings that sounded interiorly in my head. By then I was living at the pond, and it was again only three or four months before I could walk again and listen and feel what was there around me. It sustained me and I knew that it and I had worked out a relationship. Not that it knew me, but it moved and acted on me. We would not have made it together if I had been suffering in all my human relationships. I had a job that was working for me.*

*I like to live with a woman. I like to live with that woman who later joined me at the pond. She is constant surprises to me. She is a box turtle, an owl crying in the night, sun diamonding the water, and at times a chittering squirrel. But I know now if she should disappear, I could stand the solitude. Just the leaves alone could do it, I think—the three-fingered, two-fingered, one-fingered sassafras leaves, yellow, some yellow and orange, some orange. Or the large pale yellow grape leaves high up in a tree on their snake vines, their wide flatness creating a surface like the leaves of water lilies, only thinner. The leaves alone could do it. Detached, drifting down, or spiraling down, or jerking crazily up and down in the air on their way down. Next spring new ones will be up there attached again.*

From the beginning, there was no reluctance to attack Henry. In the second week, one student said, "I'm tired of this guy already. Everybody but him is doing things wrong. He's an insufferable egotist."

"Yeah, I know what you mean," said Diane. "But I'm trying not to disagree with him at this point. I know he's not perfect. He may be a great writer, but he's still just a man. I'm just trying to stay with him and find out what he thinks and how he feels. I'll suspend my judgment till later."

I was nodding my head in assent through both comments, and I said, "A friend of Henry's said she would as soon take his arm as the arm of an elm tree."

If I had answered the first speaker with Diane's thought, I believe I would have lost the seminar. Once again the teacher defending the man he has chosen to teach a course in.

As the semester progressed, again and again one or the other of us around the table would explode in exasperation or rage at Thoreau. I think we helped each other by allowing those outbursts without counterattack. Then we would read more, and someone in class would point out how Thoreau had helped him perceive. And so we achieved a rare attitude toward this man whom James Russell Lowell and Robert Louis Stevenson found so priggish and unsocial. My love for him was deepened and extended while I was instructed in more of his failings. The judiciousness of Rod's estimate, which follows, I think is representative of the blend of subjectivity and objectivity displayed by members of this seminar:

*Picked up a book on Organic Farming, hoping in some way to learn a few secrets of the "natural way." Relating this reading to you, Henry, I thought would be easy—subconsciously I thought of my grandfather (kindest man I've ever known) who dabbled in organic farming in his retirement. What I found instead was an article on homesteading in British Columbia. The story spoke of the experiences of a single young couple, living as you did off the land. The technical points concerning the short growing season, the type of lodging, the extent of their animal husbandry, all reminded me of the way in which you set out to record the particulars of your own experience with life in nature.*

*But you came off the worse for the comparison, Henry. You did not have to contend with winters whose chill reached −60°, nor worry about ground which froze to 19 feet at times. You did not have to depend upon your talents as a farmer to keep you alive day by day. If adversity in some form became too much for you, you could easily have made the relatively short trek to town—the comforts of civilization and friends within easy reach. But not so with these (I hate to use the word) hardy people.*

*You speak to us of noble things, Henry, good, pure simple things you teach us to see in nature. But these homesteaders in British Columbia (as many others before them) are taking your philosophy (though perhaps not consciously) and are living beyond it. Yours was an experiment and your commitment to it seems above reproach. But theirs is no experiment, it is permanent and their commitment is with their lives. If you can see them, Henry, I think you must smile.*

☐

As the course neared its end, I talked more and more about Thoreau's habits of revising and rewriting, of his *seven* versions of *Walden*. I asked students to revise and polish some of their best entries for possible publication of some kind. If they were to keep journals in order to understand how and what he wrote, they needed to revise them as he did. I was not thorough enough in this requirement. The students needed another semester in which to develop more self-discipline. Writing something that counts for yourself in school is an alien experience.

In the last two weeks I asked students to choose for reading aloud in class either Thoreau's long essay on wildness, called "Walking," or his essay "Life without Principle." They chose the latter. I said everyone should read the whole essay aloud to himself and be prepared to read aloud any part of it in class. Literature is a sounding art, I said, and cannot be known fully by silent readers. Then we started around the table, I reading the first two pages, Marvin the next two, and so on. I said some of them might find this a nervous task but that I thought advanced students should become good public readers. I told them that when Eleanor Roosevelt had been asked if she had ever had stage fright in giving all the speeches of her career, she had replied, "Oh, yes, I always get stage fright before I speak, but I don't let it prevent me from speaking." The reading went well, and gave us a shared ear for Thoreau's euphonious sentences.

I had also said that I expected that together we would be able to explain every word, archaic or special, and every allusion we ran up against in "Life without Principle." There was no testing of readers in this class in the formal sense, and I do not believe in holding anyone responsible for the meaning of every word in hundreds of pages assigned in classes. But this time, I said, I expected some work from everyone in that respect, so that after we had finished reading aloud, explaining, and discussing, we would be able to say that we knew one work of Thoreau's completely.

The examination of meaning was a charade. At the first session I found I was the only person who had consulted dictionaries and encyclopedias to nail down the meanings not idiomatic or contemporary for us. I quit reading the rest of the essay that closely to see what they had done on their own for our second session with the essay. They didn't do much better. One student was a confident and authoritative guesser, frequently dead wrong. Next time I try this activity I will prepare the ground more thoroughly.

☐

I have forgotten Vicki. For the record I must tell. Four weeks into the course she had written only a half dozen pages in her journal and said almost nothing at the table. I spoke to her and she said she had been considering dropping out. Two weeks later I spoke to her again when she was still saying little on paper or in class. "I just can't seem to write anything," she said. "Do you think I should drop out?" For the first time in my career I said, "That's a possible action. There's time yet to get going, but if you don't move into high gear right away, you will be cheating the class as well as yourself, for this is a seminar." Two days later I received a drop slip for her in the mail.

I had not opened her up, helped her to conquer the frightful pressure some students feel when they are expected to do more than write impersonal answers to tests and sit in a room taking lecture notes. Yet I do not feel guilty about Vicki's leaving. I don't think she was ready for the pressures of a seminar. She has the capability, but the moment has not yet arrived when she is ready to flower. Maybe it will never come for her, but the bud is there, wrapped.

I let her leave the class because several nonparticipating students can ruin a seminar. In one that is working there is a strong expectancy in the air. Students put themselves on the line when they write and talk to their peers. They expect a reciprocity.

☐

It was a brutal part of the day to meet and discuss such a dense writer as Thoreau—4:00 to 5:40, without a break. Paul wrote an entry that began:

*At 3:15 p.m. I lay down for death. My corpse was in the viewing window. At 5:30 p.m. I awoke to a new life.*

That's the way he felt about this time of the day. He added:

*Tomorrow I will be in Thoreau class during the twilight zone but I will have company for my mind and body.*

I remember frequently entering that little white room feeling leaden, looking out to see tired and hungry students. But I never remember a meeting ending with that spirit. Again and again we started slowly, and tiredly, and without being aware built up steam in the boiler until the engine was humming along. We laughed a great deal, at what students had written at a happier moment of the day, and we were lifted. In the design of this course there was freedom to play seriously, so students often played. Sam wrote:

> *Alphabet soup was a Friday standard for us little Catholic kids (the vegetable stock kind). We'd spell out bad words on soda crackers. . . . "Don't play with your food!" would bellow from somewhere and so we would eat our own words—before secretly comparing them, for status. I ate a lot of bad words. They still belch out once in a while.*
>
> *Sometimes when I cannot write what I want to, I feel like a can of alphabet soup. Plump vegetable[s] in many colors, like adjectives, slide around in the well-greased collection of letters. Everything is there—it's the unity that's lacking to make those letters into words, and words into phrases, and phrases into paragraphs, and . . . A special order to things is still needed.*
>
> *Vonnegut?—comic order out of moral chaos.*
>
> *Thurber?—matter of factness for preposterous events.*
>
> *Hemingway?—to fight the bull.*
>
> *Or maybe like Andy Warhol—Alphabet Soup is just Alphabet Soup . . . belch . . . excuse me.*

Paul kept writing in his journal short-line, concentrated, playful poems. When he wrote several paragraphs about war we urged him to make one sentence into a poem:

> *If God*
> *had wanted us*
> *to fight*
> *he would have made*
> *our skin*
> *baggy and green*
> *and our index finger*
> *capable of shooting*
> *bullets.*

Two weeks before the class ended, Paul invited the class to meet at his beautiful restored old house. We talked and ate and drank beer and read several good writings, in the most relaxed and enjoyable way. It was a totally different experience from the party held under similar circumstances in my "Free Class" described earlier. Again, I was told that several students stayed and talked for more than six hours after I left. But this time the party brought the group more closely together.

☐

The last event in the class was the reading of papers that had been written by about half the members. Early in the semester I had said that those who wanted to write a couple of factual or scholarly papers could do so. One prohibition: not in Engfish. Only one student, Sid, turned in such a paper without further prodding, and it was not strong. Half of it depended so much on its source that it might as well have been cut from the book. Later in the year I suggested that those who hadn't been producing enough in their journals might augment their work by writing one paper. I wrote my own to show them that it was possible to write idiomatically while analyzing something.

My paper was about Thoreau's metaphors. I examined some, trying to determine why they appealed to me so much more than other prose writers'. I think I found the answer: usually it is a series of short hammering sentences—some of them metaphorical—that produces Thoreau's striking power. So it is in the rhythm as well as the comparison that he scores. I wrote the paper, let it rest a few days, added to it, polished it, and thought I had something to be proud of. When I read it in class it was better received than much of my writing has been in my classes; but I realized that two of its major examples were weak. On reflection I realize that I did *not* read the paper aloud to the seminar. I feared giving them too much of me, merely passed it out dittoed. The effect of that publicity made me more critical of it. In it I had let myself be satisfied too easily. Rereading the paper at home later I concluded that my two major examples were simply invalid.

Then came the student papers—too long to reproduce here. Sam had written a fascinating explanation to Thoreau of what Irishmen are like. Earlier in class he had planted in his journal a seed for this paper:

> *Henry David, you know of the Irish but not about them. You disdain the manifestations of a complex culture. I learned of the Irish from my father—a hot tempered, violent, rotund Irishman full of confused loves and faiths. I learned in bars at the age of six; he lifted me upon the stools with his muscular arms and barreled chest and belted down Bushmills and beers by the score while I sipped my cokes and listened. My grandfather stood tall and taught my uncles, five of them, about Catholicism and booze. Once in a rainstorm he brought his friends' horse into the parlor to their overstuffed home. He taught the boys how time was only functional if you enjoyed it—to work hard and to fight together. . . .*

Now Sam opened up and told Henry about the Irish. He included a description of the breed taken from a Celtic chronicler. It was a rich, Irish stew, that paper—full of gorgeous lumps of truth. His point was not that the Irish were without fault, but rather full of fault and whiskey and fear of snakes and Henry didn't know them at all. As that seminar had proceeded, Sam had taken cues from comments on his own early writing—all of it rich—and begun to remove any fat or gristle. A little past the halfway point in the course he was turning out short pieces that seemed professional to the rest of us.

Two other papers, both about Thoreau and friendship, were deeply conceived by the writers, taken out of their needs and experiences, but curiously lacking in substance and evidence. They showed me that it was possible to work out of one's experience and commitment and still say no more than most students do in fulfilling an empty assignment. There was no time to let these two writers go back and fill in the gaps that would have made their papers powerful.

The semester was closing, and many students had to meet exorbitant demands in other classes. Several gave up to those demands altogether and quit working in the Thoreau class. But Nora came through usefully with a paper about her work in an advertising office, where a copywriter had decided to use a statement from Thoreau on the cover of a brochure about a bank. "What recommends commerce to me is its enterprise and bravery," Thoreau had written in the chapter on sounds in *Walden*. Nora laughed because she said Henry was being satirical throughout his long discussion of commerce and railroads. It was a well-organized paper and moved gracefully from Thoreau's words to Nora's experience and back. I was surprised and gratified to see it was written with conventional punctuation and capitalization and was easy to follow.

I read Nora's paper with enjoyment but then a disturbed feeling. Had Henry been putting down the railroad? I remembered his saying that he was less affected by the heroism of soldiers at Buena Vista than the railroad men going out with snowplows to keep the trains running. We reread the passages in our book and determined that Thoreau was ambivalent in speaking of the railroad and negligent in helping his reader see his divided feeling. Nora ended her paper with a fine touch: although the men at the bank thought attributing enterprise and bravery to commerce was a right notion, they could not use the quotation because Thoreau was known as a radical.

So Nora had written a paper like mine—with a vital weakness in it. I think we both learned from the experience. I hope she recognizes how good her paper was despite its flaw. It had made a way for us into Thoreau's ambiguity and it had reminded us that not everyone beyond that room considered Henry a safe man. The experience reminded me of the need for places to fail in school, and of how much could be learned if no grades except pass-fail were given in school. The chance to do something normally imperfect and not be branded for it.

Overall, this seminar did what I wanted it to. It released students to meet Thoreau on ground where they could look him in the eye. It showed them how powerful he was. It showed many of us how powerful we were. None of us had a monopoly on knowledge. We were all learning: I think Thoreau would have been too if he had been present. Not only did the students use their experience as light to throw on Thoreau's statements, but they became so suffused with his light that they saw his world becoming theirs.

Of the many things I learned from this seminar, the most touching was that the spirit of Thoreau lives in many persons today—old and young, in different parts of the world. Marvin, who had begun the course with a block on writing anything of length, finished with a three-part journal statement that entranced the rest of us:

> My grandfather owns forty acres of woodland which at present is isolated enough to be ten miles from the nearest electrical outlet. He's owned the property for sixty years. He and five other men bought the land for about $1,000, and ten years later built a cabin which still stands. To get to the cabin today it's an easy drive—if there has been no rain—off a paved road down a seldom used eight-mile mud hole called a logging road, and then half a mile hike to their nest. But sixty years ago the mud hole wasn't there. They had to drive to a place five miles north of their property and come down stream by boat. Fortunately the stream cuts right through the middle of their land. That's where their dwelling stands, along the Big Two-Hearted River.
>
> The trip down five miles of stream is a toilsome and onerous task, the river is too shallow for a motor, too narrow to use oars and fallen trees and stumps in the water would make it a very wet trip if you were foolish enough to try a canoe. They had to pole their way down, a method which is slow and tiresome if done on a stump-filled, log-jammed meandering stream, such as the Big Two-Hearted. If not done with care, a lot of balance, and a tremendous amount of teamwork, an unexpected bath is your reward.
>
> They would haul in their lumber and tools on a couple of boats and then turn around and go back for another load. One ten-hour, round-trip ordeal a day was all they could handle. My brothers and I used to kid my grandfather about how long it took to travel those meager ten miles. We felt we could do it in half the time, so we tried it. We don't kid him any more. I was 20, my brother 22, prime of life, or so we thought. We departed at 6:00 in the morning and arrived back, very tired, very hungry, very wet, and most of all very humble at 8:00 that night.
>
> Because of the responsibilities of families and jobs, and because of the length of the trip, they could make it only twice a

year for a stay of a week or two at a time. It took them five years to complete the cabin. It's simple but it looked a mansion to them. It's a two-room lodge, three if you count the bathroom that stands fifty feet away. Inside, the kitchen and dining areas are separated from the sleeping and living quarters. There are sleeping accommodations for eight. Two large bunk type beds lined with straw mattresses, not comfortable but welcome after a long day of fishing, hiking, hunting, or working with an ax or saw. On the opposite side of the room stands a large round table where fifty years of beer, chilled by the Big Two-Hearted River, and good sweet sippin' bourbon has been poured, fifty years of tales about the big buck or black bear that never was seen, let alone shot at, were told; and fifty years of black-jack, seven-card stud, and five-card draw have been played. From the rafters hung their wet socks and boots and on the walls calendars fifteen or twenty years old, with pictures of that never-seen buck or black bear being shot at by men other than them. The pictures represent their dreams of that once-in-a-life-time chance of bagging a real trophy.

In the other room is the kitchen, indoor water pump, sink, shelves for dishes and glasses, and a large, ominous looking stove. It is an old wood burning stove at least twice the size of any of those modern ones used today. My grandfather is proud of it, not because he is fond of cooking on it—which he is—but because he was the one who brought it downstream, 500 pounds of oven and stove down five miles of river in a boat.

How many eggs and steaks must have been cooked on that stove over the fifty years? Across from that monster sits a counter where countless numbers of onions, carrots, and celery have been sliced and chopped for those steaks and on the shelves above sit the dishes and glasses. Each of the group had his own glass with his name on it. My grandfather's is the only one still used. His sits by itself on another shelf. The others are together on a different one, the owners long since dead.

Steaks well done, eggs sunnyside up, orange juice and strong black coffee, sometimes mixed with a little of the poison that had cut them down the night before used as an antidote to bring alive dulled senses. These were served on long planks set on carpenter's horses that acted as their dining table, which took up the other half of the kitchen area. Breakfast done, dishes washed, faces scraped clean of beards 24 hours old, possibly a bath, for those brave enough, in the frigid water of the Big Two-Hearted, my grandfather and his friends would then go about their work, hunting, fishing, hiking, or working to correct any flaws in their wooden castle. If they had reason to cross over to the other side of the river, they would walk down a fairly steep embankment to the stream (the cabin sat on the top of a small hill which overlooked their domain) and cross by means of the bridge they had built.

The bridge was constructed the first year they were there, sixty years ago. It's still used, but it's a precarious crossing, one done with a little care. When they built it, they dragged three forty-foot logs down the hill to the water and suspended them from bank to bank over the stream. They held each to the others by nailing slats across them at intervals. They then built railings, which assured a safe and dry crossing of the river, by driving small logs into the sandy bottom of the stream and connecting them with other small logs. The bridge has weathered well considering the weight of time and people it has had to withstand. Two of the three larger logs that span the river have since rotted and broken and lie in the river, leaving only the one to suffer the weight of travelers, and the railings have been bleached white by the sun and are wobbly and not to be trusted.

This is the first year in sixty that my grandfather has not been to his lodge in the Upper Peninsula, and he will never go again. He is just too old and tired. My brothers and I own it now, and our work is to begin soon. New logs will be cut to replace those broken on the bridge and the railings that cozen travelers into using them only to find them untrustworthy will be tightened and made solid and reliable again. A new cabin will be built, not as a replacement for the old, but rather as a labor to enjoy and rejoice over when completed.

Land will be cleared and prepared near the lake created by the beavers who constructed the dam on a small tributary of the Big Two-Hearted. Their lodges are on the water, as are the homes of several varieties of ducks and geese, and a large integrated school system of trout and bass. Around the lake is a network of thoroughfares used by deer. If one takes an exit off the highway across the dam, a ghetto of bears' winter residences will be seen, apparently among the few in the community who are well enough off not to have to work during the winter months. Construction begins next summer on our cabin along the edge of the lake, a new addition in town. We are of a different denomination, but I think we will be accepted. It will take years to build our place, but we will be rewarded for our pains and pleasures the same way that my Thoreau-ean grandfather was.

Marvin's account told us once again, more powerfully, what we had concluded around the table: Thoreau's two years at the cabin was a relatively civilized venture. We knew that he could walk the short distance through the woods to a home-cooked meal whenever he wanted one. Family and friends were always close. The Walden area sustained no bears, presented Thoreau with no herculean challenges of survival. I believe we suffered the initial shock of understanding that our man was living a life of refinement, however simple. And then, with the tolerance that comes from knowing something well over a long period of time, we came back to admiring Henry. He had found a way of enjoying the best of two worlds, of making his love his work (as he advocated), of spending his mornings writing or surveying and his afternoons walking. What he wanted to do was write, read, and study nature. He exerted the least possible effort getting to these activities day after day, year after year. As Emerson said, "he had in a short life [forty-four years] exhausted the capabilities of the world"—I would add, "for rendering to him what was his."

☐

In this course I had overcome the weakness of the Free Class I described earlier. Here the students brought themselves and their opinions to the table and made them illuminate the writings of one man, that cranky, eloquent, sharp-eyed, narrow fellow who was as deep as Walden Pond. Together we heard his words and our words speaking to each other. There was diversity and unity in that room—a polarity that crackled.

## Chapter 6

# Leo and Lucius

☐

... the separation of man as subject from the field of objective nature blinds him to the form of life proper to him. Man can only fully understand himself by fusing the objective knowledge which is gained by observation of the whole of organic nature with the subjective knowledge of individual experience. This can bring a new ease and self-acceptance, an innocence based on knowledge.

Lancelot Law Whyte, *The Next Development in Man*
(New York: Henry Holt & Company, 1948), p. 223.

□

These days when I speak of other teachers, I often sound uncharitable. I hope that I am equally uncharitable when I consider my own teaching.

Those two sentences suggest I may have become perverted. Why could I not simply say that I will be *charitable* toward all teachers who are trying, including myself?

I have learned it is too easy for teachers to excuse themselves. When they do that unjustly, every student in their classes suffers—and regularly, at 1:00 P.M. Monday, Wednesday, and Friday if they are in college or high school; or from 8:00 to 3:00 for five days of the week if they are in elementary school. A comparison with a chain gang is not inaccurate. If the men are suffering, will the overseer deny responsibility?

I now ask of every teacher only one thing: are your students doing good works? There is no other test of a teacher.

Since I have found that test—the only one I want to see administered in schools, and one which itself shuns those devices customarily called "tests"—I have begun to locate the great teachers in my experience. I have already furnished a portrait of Jesse Mack. Here I wish to add two more portraits and begin a gallery.

Leo Tolstoy was working in 1862 and I found him by reading. Lucius Garvin was working in 1939 and I found him by signing up for his class. Leo was explosive and emotional in demeanor, Lucius contained. Leo was a great artist who found control and objectivity when he sat down to write; Lucius was not known to the general public but found his humanity when he sat down with his students. Both enabled their students to do work that astounded them.

□

## Leo Tolstoy

In his beautiful book *The Lives of Children* George Dennison says the question is not "How can we improve our schools?" but "How can we educate our young?" He is warning those reformers who may waste their hours on surface changes. Other reformers believe that valuable learning will occur only when schools are abolished or education "deschooled." My recent experience tells me that inside or outside schools the central question should be, "How can we get other persons to do and think things that count for them, for us, and for others?" Education can be fruitless or fruitful in both casual and highly structured situations.

In *The Lives of Children* George Dennison mentions the school that Leo Tolstoy founded on his own estate for the children of his serfs. Tolstoy tells, in *Tolstoy on Education* (Chicago: University of

Chicago Press, 1967), how he discovered new ways of teaching. Once he read a proverb to the children and asked them to write on it. They decided the task was beyond them and one child said to Tolstoy, "Write it yourself." So he started in and soon two boys joined him. Soon the other boys began looking into his story and asking him about it. They made suggestions. He found his ideas for the story were more artificial than theirs. Eventually most of the boys took part in the writing. One, Fédka, excelled at determining what should be put in and left out of the story. When he became despotic, all the other boys left except Sémka.

Tolstoy worked with these two boys from seven until eleven that night, the three of them arguing what was organic to the story and true to life. Tolstoy was amazed at their inventions, especially Fédka's suggestion that the sickly, narrow-chested, gossiping man should suddenly put on a woman's fur coat. It was this detail that early established the story for Tolstoy as profoundly right and human. They worked on the story for three days in the class. By accident the manuscript was destroyed, but they began it again and finished it. One page of the original was later found. When Tolstoy prepared the story for publication in the magazine of the school, he combined both variants. "I only wrote out the title, divided the story into chapters, and here and there corrected the mistakes, which were due to carelessness." [p. 206]

Today as I sat out in the bright May sunshine, looking down the road which parallels the small lake on which I live, I was astounded by the depth of shadow and light in the scrub trees and bush in the new woods. I looked back to Tolstoy's pages and found them equally surprising. I was reading a man telling one hundred and ten years ago of a teaching experience that almost exactly repeated mine. I like to say it that way for it suggests that the most powerful experiences arise individually for women and men. Thinking chronologically, I could say my experience repeated Tolstoy's, but it makes no difference. The two were not sequential.

Our only difference was that Tolstoy began his teaching of writing by writing the first page of a story and I begin mine by asking my students for free writing. From then on, everything is the same. I am amazed by the ability of my students to put down truths unique and surprising, by the way the habit of telling truths springs them loose from trite and verbose expression, by their willingness to criticize my writing (which I sometimes bring into the classroom) with candor and penetration.

Tolstoy was teaching peasants—the last persons in his time who would be expected to possess the powers he found in them. It was the finished story which moved Tolstoy, not a hopeful notion about what divine young children might accomplish. And he published it. And it counted for his students, himself, and other readers. I am teaching middle-class students in a state-supported university of 21,000 students in

Kalamazoo, Michigan, the last place many persons in this country would expect to find a large number of thoughtful and perceptive persons.

Today it is common for professional persons to look to the ghettos for exciting proof of the power of new teaching methods. If a black child writes for his whole composition,

> *I'm telling you that Ben is some dude. Yesterday he sold $500 worth of shit to a kid who washes the windows for the Baptist preacher.*

This work is apt to be praised as bold and brilliant writing when in fact it is only a beginning. The related facts create some tension and surprise, but the dude is not revealed sufficiently. The style is competent but not memorable. These are perhaps the first truths got down on paper by a boy who might learn to write powerfully. But if a teacher comes up with no more than a collection of undeveloped writings of this kind in his class, he has not got out of his students what Tolstoy and a number of high-school and college teachers in the country whom I know are now getting out of theirs. Tolstoy was not satisfied with dreams of transmuting dirty peasant boys into angels or geniuses. He wanted performance.

I remarked upon the similarities of our experience. Tolstoy summarized the successful methods which he had stumbled upon in trying to teach writing. They are exactly the methods I found, knowing nothing at the time of his experience. Tolstoy says:

(1) Give a great variety of themes, not inventing them specially for the children, but propose such as appear most serious and interesting to the teacher himself.

(2) Give the children children's compositions to read, and give them only children's compositions as models, for children's compositions are always more correct, more artistic, and more moral than the compositions of grown people. [I do not go along with what appears there after the word *for.*]

(3) (Most important.) When looking through a pupil's composition, never make any remarks to him about the cleanliness of the copy-book, nor about penmanship, nor orthography, nor, above all, about the structure of the sentences and about logic.

(4) Since the difficulty of composition does not lie in the volume, nor the contents, nor the artistic quality of the theme, the sequence of the themes is not to be based on volume, nor on the contents, nor on the language, but in the mechanism of the work, which consists, first, in selecting one out of a large number of ideas and images presented; secondly, in choosing words for it and clothing it in words; thirdly, in remembering it and finding a place for it; fourthly, in not repeating nor leaving out anything,

and in the ability of combining what follows with that which precedes, all the time keeping in mind what is already written down; fifthly, and finally, in thinking and writing at the same time, without having one of these acts interfere with the other. . . .

At the end of his explanation, Tolstoy records the objections to his teaching which he commonly heard. They are the same as I hear to mine.

. . . We shall be told: "You, the teacher, may unconsciously, to yourself, have helped in the composition of these stories, and it would be too difficult to find the limits of that which belongs to you, and of that which is original."

We shall be told: "We shall admit that the story is good, but that it is only one kind of literature."

We shall be told: "Fédka and the other boys, whose compositions you have printed, are happy exceptions."

We shall be told: "You are yourself a writer, and, without knowing it, you have been helping the pupils along paths which cannot be prescribed as a rule to other teachers who are not authors themselves."

We shall be told: "From all that it is impossible to deduce a common rule or theory. It is partially an interesting phenomenon, and nothing else."

Having heard these objections many times myself when I talk to groups of teachers or students around the country, I was not surprised to see them dated 1862. They arise from the fear and guilt of teachers. Sometimes teachers sense that their students' work is boring them and each other. It would bore outsiders if the teachers had the courage to show it to them. Sometimes they are shown by reformers student work that is alive, and the difference unsteadies them. And it should, for it threatens their whole professional lives.

The five objections Tolstoy gives above are all designed to absolve the teacher. They imply that Tolstoy's success was a mistake, an accident, a phenomenon due to unusual circumstances. I know why teachers raise these cries. Today I am more aware than ever of the need to preserve my self-respect if my teaching goes wrong. For now I know that most of the middle-class students in the typical midwestern university where I teach are talented and perceptive. They have proved so in my classes. Only last semester I found myself reaching for rationalizations like those Tolstoy lists—when I considered the first weak Shakespeare class I have taught in six years.

## Lucius Garvin

In my undergraduate days at Oberlin College I had three powerful teachers—about average I believe, three out of forty. One was Lucius Garvin, a handsome young philosophy professor who taught a sophomore course titled Ethics. We had a textbook. It was red, but I don't remember for sure what was in it. We read ethical philosophy for each meeting and when we came to class Mr. Garvin would tell a little story of real, crucial experience which was easy for us to identify with. Then we would speculate on what the philosopher for that week might have said about that experience.

Mr. Garvin was enabling us to probe and understand our judgments of human experience. He arranged things so that the nine of us in that class made connections between the philosophical generalizations we had just read and the particulars of a happening. I can hear a skeptic saying that anyone could teach with only nine students. Not most persons I have known who occupied the front of the room and called themselves teacher.

In Ethics class we did the same thing every day for the whole semester and never became bored. The expected was there—we knew what we were going to be asked to do with our reading; so we read accordingly, to understand so we could apply. And the unexpected—our individual reactions to the experience Mr. Garvin related. He asked us what the philosopher of the day would say about the action we were discussing, but that question usually occurred toward the end of each period, and sometimes never at all. Our principal act was to say what *we* thought would be the good choice of action (ethical—the point of this course was never lost) in the situations. So we were constantly talking of our own experience as we put ourselves into the one before the class. I am not sure whether Mr. Garvin began the course that way or intended it to go that way, but it soon did; and he did nothing to prevent the drift. He enjoyed the class, and the others and I soon felt we were taking a course in making moral decisions. Every day we were being tested as we took the responsibility for thinking our way through to these decisions. I don't remember any quizzes or exams until the final exam, and that, I believe, was more of the same decision making.

Soon we began to see that our teacher always analyzed the situation (after we had our chance, never before) from the point of view of a Utilitarian. He called the position Hedonistic, and woke us up with that word our mothers and fathers had always used as a synonym for *sinful.*

One day he admitted he was taking the Utilitarian position as if he were a Hedonist so we could see what it meant day after day to bring our ideas up against a person who believed in a position and had thought it out carefully. For a while I supposed he was doing this as a gambit, but the more I heard, the more I suspected he believed in it firmly. Years later I realized what it had meant to me to listen daily to a man who had a comprehensive view of the world, who genuinely possessed standards and employed them steadfastly albeit with an openness to change.

We were hearing from a Utilitarian, who was practicing what the greatest of Utilitarians, John Stuart Mill, preached:

> Nor is it enough that he should hear the arguments of adversaries from his own teachers, presented as they state them, and accompanied by what they offer as refutations. That is not the way to do justice to the arguments, or bring them into real contact with his own mind. He must be able to hear them from persons who actually believe them; who defend them in earnest, and do their very utmost for them. [*On Liberty* (New York: Appleton-Century-Crofts, 1947), p. 36.]

Almost all my other professors acquainted me with the accepted ideas in their fields, presenting them as objectively as possible, and I got the notion that ideas were to be handled but not made part of me.

I remember being a little frightened in that Ethics class for the first two-thirds of the semester. Here I was wriggling and clutching at and then withdrawing from a real test—putting my convictions on the line and noting what experts in that strange art had said about difficult choices. At first I didn't talk much. It was almost too much for me and some of the others. Mr. Garvin made it hard for us. And he made it easy. It was a small class; if one of us didn't speak for days upon end, the fact would be noticed by everyone else in the room. So he didn't call on us individually. He waited for us to speak, and we did.

If we oversimplified life, Mr. Garvin showed us it was complex. A story he told about Abraham Lincoln has stuck with me for over thirty-five years. He said it was apocryphal. Lincoln and a friend were riding along a muddy road, their carriage wheels sinking in the spring ooze, when they heard a pig squealing.

"I think it's stuck in the fence," said Lincoln's friend.

They rode on fifty yards and Lincoln kept turning in the direction of the noise and squirming in his seat. He drove another fifty yards, suddenly stopped the horses and got out. There was no turning around in that mud.

"I have to go back and free that pig," he said churlishly.

When the pig's squeals ceased and Lincoln returned, he said to his friend, "I'll bet you think I went back because I felt sorry for the pig. The fact is that it was a selfish act. I couldn't stand that squealing any longer and so to make myself comfortable, I freed him."

"I don't think that's true," said his friend.

"Well, it certainly is," said Lincoln, "No man is all that unselfish, least of all me."

"I think if you reflect long enough, you will conclude that you went back there because you couldn't stand the noise and also because you felt sorry for the pig."

My Shakespeare students and I have learned this truth from *Hamlet* and *Romeo and Juliet*. We argue about why a character did this or that and soon find ourselves seeing that men and women usually act upon many motives, seldom upon one.

In those days I sensed little about Mr. Garvin's methods. All I knew was that when I entered that room, I plunged into a dizzying conversation about life which suspended all my thought about everything else in that lonely and largely disheartening experience of my first two years at college. It was a decade later before I realized that Lucius Garvin had been one of the three or four agents in my life who had taught me to think. In the previous thirteen grades of school I had been given the word. It was from out there, hence objective, I was sure. I had no notion that a word from me—except in rote answer—might have a place against The Word. The subjective and the objective together? It was years before I would understand the significance of that juxtaposition, but Mr. Garvin had already given me some of its fruits.

☐

My failure in teaching that Senior Seminar reminds me of a fact I often forget. I have learned to move students from success to success so that they begin to exercise their natural powers—to command their experience, to inquire steadily, to make fruitful connections. And I have seen how they can sustain, encourage, and bring out the best in each other. But jealousy and mutual discouragement are also natural to human beings. Once begun, the movement from failure to failure becomes habitual. I should have this truth before me constantly. In my home, I regret to say, the members of my family often carp and rail, rub each other the wrong way. When my wife and I and our two daughters spent a year in Mexico and conducted a relatively free school at home, we made sure our class hours were full of encouragement. Then we often met each other at our best. Outside of class, we often met at our worst.

Mr. Garvin recognized this danger. When we did not bring our best thoughts to the discussion, he waited and listened, and then before the end of the hour gave us some of his insights on the matter at hand. When we spoke well, he sat back and admired us.

## Chapter 7

# A General Education Course

☐

[Thoreau] would not offer a memoir of his observations to the Natural History Society. "Why should I? To detach the description from its connections in my mind would make it no longer true or valuable to me: and they do not wish what belongs to it."

Ralph Waldo Emerson, "Thoreau"

□

Several years ago I attended a public lecture by Charles Van Riper, a speech therapist at Western Michigan University who is visited by persons from all over the world who want to attain the power of speech or be relieved of stuttering. He was talking to a staff of teachers in the School of General Education. He began by praising the concept of General Education and then told how as a young man he had got into his field, which at the time was no field at all. He was a stutterer. One day, frustrated and driven, near suicide, he walked alone to a wood in the Northern Peninsula of Michigan. Unknowingly he had come there to make a decision: would he give up, or would he conquer his infirmity at any cost? He found himself swearing that he would do anything necessary to enter the world of men and become a person of value. He did a little dedicatory dance around a birch tree there alone in the woods.

So he began to focus on stuttering. He read encyclopedias, biology texts, anything that might help him understand what a person does mechanically and psychologically that creates stuttering. He studied psychology, philosophy, medicine. In field after field he became versed enough to see how the facts and principles in that discipline supplemented or contradicted each other in furthering his pursuit. As he began to make a new discipline—speech therapy—he was becoming more specialized. And yet to do that he had ranged widely and generally.

When he sat down after his moving, vivid talk, the audience of General Education teachers and administrators applauded vigorously. I smiled, thinking that the applause was for a man who had shown that his productive course moved in the opposite direction from most General Education courses. He went down through the particular act of stuttering and out into other fields, taking a general tour, and then back to the special problem again. But the movements were combined, or alternated, and they centered in one man who was acting upon a single urge.

□

I am tempted to say that every General Education course should be specialized and every specialized course should be generalized. I guess I will say that. It is simplistic, but useful.

□

To go beyond that statement I will now present my experiences teaching a General Education course called Criticism of Mass Media. I felt qualified to teach it. For about ten years I had taught at Michigan

State University in a department dedicated to the study and practice of communication, written a doctoral dissertation on objectivity and responsibility in newspaper reporting, and had been observing mass communication closely for about twenty-five years. When I moved to San Francisco State College in 1960, I stipulated that I must be given a course in the mass media. Since then, I've taught that course many times. Up until last year, I would call it a failure. Only two or three of my students in each class became excited and seemed to learn something.

At the end of the semester in San Francisco I received the most negative evaluations of my teaching I had ever seen. Half the class thought the course a waste of time. I felt that to make the students better judges of what they encountered in the media, I had to give them some of my judgments. They frequently resisted them. I could sense animosity growing. The critical papers the students wrote seldom illuminated a mass communication.

Each year in that course I have tried new techniques. Slowly I moved from trying to feed students a lot of knowledge—through books and lectures—to forcing them to make critical studies on their own of aspects of mass communication that interested them. To teach them how pictures speak to each other and what editing does to them, I had each student construct a slide show or film. The project ate up a third of the course time. A few of the brightest students did good work and increased their ability to perceive movies and television programs. But more than half of the class made a botch of their project and learned little. (I'm aware of the slipperiness of the term I just used—"brightest students." It usually means those who come closest to thinking and talking like the teacher.)

The spread was too much in that class. To take up thoroughly any one of the media—film, television, newspapers, magazines—in fifteen weeks was impossible, much less all four. The trouble with that General Education course, like most others in the College of General Studies, was that it was too general.

In that course I intended to accomplish one thing if nothing else—to correct the jaundiced view of news reporting that most students adopt as a result of listening to college professors. I had taken it on myself in the years before World War II. Hitler and Goebbels were using the mass media to poison the minds of Germans and other people over the world. On the radio and in newspapers and magazines they repeated the big lie. In this country the Institute of Propaganda Analysis was founded by liberals who saw the need to teach Americans to see through the tricks of the propagandists. Partly under the influence of S. I. Hayakawa and his book *Language in Action*, young instructors came to believe that almost all communications were maliciously slanted or biased. At Columbia University Paul Lazarsfeld carried out extensively what was called a "content analysis" of mass communications. It was too often a counting of what the researcher had predetermined was a cue showing bias on the part of the communicator. Little of the human difficulties of perceiving and reporting truth was revealed.

In my doctoral study I tried to find out what it was like for a human being to report human actions. I made case histories of newspaper and television reporters from the moment they got their assignment until their communication reached the public. I found that indeed every man's perceptions of an event are colored by his past experience—including that of the most responsible and knowledgeable reporters. And scientists, and medical doctors, and professors. But the best men often conquered their biases as well as gave into them. And the whole act was a hundred times more exacting and thrilling than the content analysts suggested. The most rigorous, unbiased, and responsible scholar I have ever met was Peter Kihss, a working reporter of *The New York Times*, whom I followed one day while he tried to report fairly and responsibly a sham investigative hearing conducted by a senator trying to get headlines by opening up mail coming into the Port of New York from Communist countries.

I wanted to get my students to learn what I had learned. In the Mass Media course I tried asking them to write news reports of events on campus or in town that they thought would probably be covered in a local newspaper. Then they were to compare their report with that of a professional.

The assignment never worked. I seldom received anything but laughably inaccurate and incomplete reports. When I compared them to professional work, the students were hurt and angry. I was expecting them to compete with professionals? They forgot all about learning from comparison. Since this project was written and took a good bit of their time, I had to grade it. Otherwise it would not have had academic sanction. Many students would have skipped the assignment if I was not going to grade it. Each year I hesitated to try that reporting assignment again. Each year I felt I had to. It made sense. Maybe something would happen to make it work. It didn't.

During a sabbatical year in Mexico I thought about how to teach that unsuccessful class. I determined I was going to try once more and if I didn't do well, I would quit teaching it and spend time talking and writing against General Education courses that involved large surveys of human experience.

☐

When I returned in the fall I was through teaching students to sit like slugs while I tried to show them the importance of evaluating the mass communications that shaped so much of their world. I would make them perceptive critics. The principal act would be to write criticisms of mass communications. But they thought they couldn't write, and they thought they didn't know anything about mass media. Many of them were too busy studying or partying to read newspapers and magazines or look at television. And films cost too much to attend frequently.

I told the students that anyone could write if he was honest. And that writing down whatever came to their minds for a few minutes would release them from the academic straitjacket. I talked a while about Engfish, the say-nothing, feel-nothing dialect of the schools, encouraged them to get some talk into their writing but not the flab that curses our conversation, words like *really, of course,* and *you know.* I told them to write freely for half an hour, turn in their papers, and leave. One girl wrote:

> *I think I say "really" too much. When people say something I always say, "Oh, really?" even when I know that it's the truth. I guess I say it because I don't know what else to say and am not a very good conversationalist with people I don't know very well.*
>
> *I really (see?) surprised myself in my A & V class today. We had to say something about ourselves and I got scared, but when it got my turn I sounded pretty good. Then the teacher asked me another question later on and I talked for a little while, but all of a sudden my mind went blank and I just couldn't think of another thing to say or even finish the sentence I was on. After three and a half years of school I still have never said very much in any of my classes. I get scared and think that I am always wrong—or else I just can't think of anything to say at all—so I just sit and try to look in a way that will make the instructor not call on me. Some instructors say that they call on the ones that don't look them in the eye, so I try to look at them but at the last minute I always look away.*
>
> *I really (again) don't quite understand that part of myself. I can be so loud and confident and funny sometimes and so shy, scared, and dumb feeling other times. Sometimes I try to be confident at a time when I'm really scared, but I get shot down and my mind goes blank on me. Not really blank, but just not able to think of an answer to the question being asked. I can think of lots of other things but not what is being discussed. I think that's why most kids hate General Studies classes. If you're not a born talker, you're out of it because they are mostly discussion—and your grade depends partly on what you say out loud in class. Not what you think but never have the confidence to say.*

This passage may be marred by the excessive use of the words *just* and *really* but it shows precisely what happens to a student who has passed through the school system being questioned by teacher and for three and a half years listening to lectures. Her mind is "Not really blank, but just not able to think of an answer to the question being asked." The traditional teacher's response to that remark is, "She is rationalizing. She doesn't know the answer to the question." I have learned that it is not the answer that is inadequate but the question, the very fact of its being there prevents the student from having a question or thought of her own. Something about this review of her school life makes her uncomfortable, but she does not understand clearly that she is all there, complete with thoughts and experience, and the system is disabling her. It is my job to help her bring herself alive in the university classroom.

□

I had told the students to write on anything that came to their minds. Nick Kekic had returned to the university after a year off working and traveling on his own.

*I put on that old teapot plus four pieces of toast in the toaster. In the morning everything is such a hassle. It seems getting together all the necessary elements for breakfast takes forever, the butter, teabags, spoon, sugar, cup, paper towel. And it always happens—the boiling $H_2O$ and toast mature at the same time. Well, I'd put the teabag in the cup, pour the hot sizzling water, making sure that the teabag string stayed hanging outside the cup.*

*Then I took care of the toast, four pieces of white filler. Finally the tea and bread converged on the table into a meal. This is when the despair thoughts would run through my mind: eight hours of boredom for a menial wage, hassles over nothing. Thoughts of school would enter the think box: "Ah, getting up early at school won't be difficult at all."*

*I was wrong, it's still hard although there are many differences between the two gettingsups. When the alarm rang this morning, no thoughts of saying the hell with it entered my head. Oh, maybe taking an extra half hour of sleep was suggested, but that's it. After all the contemplation of taking the extra time is over, you have usually wasted ten minutes already and have been on the verge of unintentionally falling back to sleep. Then suddenly you just jump out of bed. At school, I always take a shower in the morning. I never did before a day of work. . . .*

*I'm ready for the school work. After vagabonding for so long, it will be good to have something concrete to rely on—like a bed and a decent meal.*

*Made dinner of canned spaghetti. I can see the routine forming. Into the room and the contemplation begins: what to eat? An examination of cans is needed, although really you know what's there. But what the hell, looking makes it more fun. Finally the selection and anticipation. Hmmmm, when was the last time I had that? San Diego? S.F.? It's a long way. You forget about food and start thinking about the odyssey. You even have a different perspective on food now. The reveries end and you get back to work.*

*The can opener. It's a good one, the top comes off almost too easily. No hassle. Dump the contents into the pan, and then the walk to the hot plate room. A few minutes of standing, fiddling commences.*

*Finally, after four tastes it's hot enough. Back to the room. A paper plate is pulled out and the meal begins.*

When I read Nick's quickly written narrative, he ceased to be simply another student. He had a life of his own and was reflecting on it. I thought of the varied and rich dinners Joyce had been serving lately at home and then of his choice among cans.

On that first day, Cathy Carlson wrote:

*Well, this assignment sounds easy enough, just hope I don't get too big a callus on my finger—they're so ugly, maybe only because it's compared to the rest of skin which is so beautiful. Can anyone completely callous their body? What would it look like if it started to peel? Hell, it would take forty-eight hours to peel it all off—whoever can do it without breaking its continuousness (as in an apple) is the winner. Underneath would be so sensitive, raw nerve endings. Such excruciating pain to get a sunburn like that. I can't take pain. That worries me—what if I'm captured? I'll talk before they even threaten me. How could those martyrs do it?*

Some of the other free writings bored me, but there were enough lively ones to be read to the class as strong signs of the wit and perception that resided in those students, most of whom had chosen this course in order to fulfill a General Education requirement.

☐

At the next meeting I asked the students to begin writing freely in journals their responses to any mass communication that had struck them in the last few days. There would be no tests. We would read a book (Lillian Ross's *Picture*, a case history of the making of John Huston's film *The Red Badge of Courage*), look at some newspapers and films together, watch a few commercial television shows if the TV cable was installed in our new classroom building in time, and I would present some of my experience and ideas. I would let them grade themselves in the course, so the act of writing could not penalize any person.

I didn't want to do that. I knew if they all gave themselves a "B," the class grades would skew the grading curve in the university. An injustice. I compared that to the unfairness of teaching a General Education course to persons not interested in or prepared for analyzing the mass media. And to the unfairness of asking students to pay money for a course that bored them and taught them nothing.

I figured that without grades half the students would cut class a good share of the time. When the semester ended, I estimated that absences were lower than in classes I had taught the conventional way.

I had thought students wouldn't write much. I received slightly more writing than in conventional classes. From about ten of the twenty-eight students I received some journal entries that taught everyone in class, including me. From the rest I received writing that touched crucial issues, so I could use them as springboards for discussion.

Most of the journal entries were short, 100 to 300 words. Scrawled on the page they looked trivial, and since I was trying a bold experiment with this class, they made me uneasy. Here's a sample:

> *I've been watching* The Mike Douglas Show *for a period of time. Used to enjoy him and his entertaining but there is something that he does which really annoys me. When he talks with his guests he asks such dumb questions, sometimes they're almost embarrassing. For instance he'll ask a comedian if he thinks he is funny. What more can the comedian say but "Yes" or "Well, I hope so"? I don't know if Douglas's writers are that bad or if he just runs out of things to ask his guests. Another thing Mike Douglas does is to cut his guests' answers short. It's as if he crams so many questions into a few minutes. I don't even think he is interested or half of the time even listening to what they have to say.*

The comment is short and undeveloped, but it shows why television talk shows produce discomfort in some sensitive viewers. Like the two journal entries that follow, it takes the reader far enough into the communication being commented on that the reader can begin to judge the writer's judgments, an essential in any criticism. Because the class was being conducted as a seminar, the need to do this became apparent when students' journal entries were read to the class. It was this sort of discipline that I did not bring about in my Senior Seminar documented earlier in this book.

It is not easy to say what makes one television comedy show superior to another. Early in the course, Carol DeMoor, who wrote the next two entries, showed us how to do that.

### 1

> *I watched* The Mary Tyler Moore Show *last night. It was the first show of the new season. I could tell because there was new music and some new pictures during the credits. I've been fairly impressed with that show every time I've seen it. The characters*

*are real people. Even though I am usually sure of what they'll do and say—how they'll react, I still think they're well created, really multi-dimensional.*

*Anyway, last night the show started out the morning after a special that Mary had done on her TV station. She works in a newsroom. This could be written a lot more concisely. And should be. One of her friends, Phyllis, tells her how much her whole family enjoyed watching "What's Your Sexual IQ?" Phyllis decides it's time to tell her 8th grade daughter the facts of life, but can't bring herself to do it. She's kind of a rattlehead who gets away with pulling some real shit on Mary and still not being hated too much. So since Mary had produced this sex show, Phyllis asks her to tell her daughter. So Mary's worried and wants to make sure she handles it just right. All this lead-up stuff is kind of pat, raunchy humor; but it's still funny enough to tolerate. So Saturday morning comes when Mary is supposed to tell the little girl (I forget her name) all about "it."*

*Mary tells her that she wants to talk to her about love. "Oh good, I've wanted to ask Phyllis." (She calls her mother by her first name.) "But you know how she is." Now I remember. The girl's name is Beth. Beth says she has a boy friend who says he loves her but she doesn't know if she can love him back. Somehow in the course of the discussion, the terms* love *and* sex *get used interchangeably by Mary, to which Beth responds by asking, "Which are we talking about?"*

*Then there's really a great scene where Beth turns her back on Mary and talks about her feelings toward her boy friend. It is obvious from this that she is afraid if she tells that boy she loves him, then sex will follow automatically. What she is saying is she does not want to have intercourse with him. This is really a moving scene, really well done, really realistic. I've never seen anything on the subject of telling one's children about "the birds and the bees" handled so sensitively, least of all on TV. But this was great.*

2

*Incidentally, there is another super-funny character on this show—Rhoda Morgenstern. She's like this (1) pushing thirty (2) not married (3) no prospects (4) always looking (5) beautiful (6) but a little heavy (7) able to laugh at her own situation (which I interpret as real inner contentment). She tells Mary not to give Beth any books to read about sex. "That's what my mother handed me. And somehow I always had the idea that I'd have to swim up the Columbia River." Funny. (And on TV.)*

Carol's comments showed me that at least one student already had the critical powers I wanted to develop in this class. She could teach the others, and possibly me. How many others were her equals or were as perceptive but not as articulate? To some extent, I could find out by reading her comments and assessing the other students' responses. I now see that a teacher must quickly arrange things so that students reveal themselves at their best. If I had spent most of the first days lecturing, I wouldn't have learned what I should expect of this class, where I should start, how far I should aim to stretch my students.

☐

When I first began teaching a course in mass media, I spent a great deal of time on the favorite subject of sociologically oriented professors: the power of the media to stultify its audiences. Early in this class I received a journal entry which did the job shortly and more refreshingly than I had customarily done it.

> On the back of my tube of Crest is a saying that used to be aired several times a day. Since the tube was all squeezed up, I could see only a few words, but knowing it was Crest, and having seen the commercial at least a million—no two million times, I was able to run through it without a single mistake. The phrase is "Crest has beeen shown to be an effective decay-preventing dentifrice that can be of significant value when used in a conscientiously applied program of oral hygiene and regular professional care." Whoever thought TV is not addicting?

Several years ago I would have taken that entry and used it as one of several examples in a little lecture on TV's powers of stupefaction. At this moment in the mass media class I simply read the entry to the class and asked if anyone wanted to add examples of their own. Two persons did. There was no need for me to talk at length.

☐

Now many of my students surprise me and their comments make my work easier. I am refreshed and so are they. In this class every student read Lillian Ross's *Picture*, in which director John Huston played a large role. Late in the semester a girl turned in this journal entry.

> LOOK. *An article on a John Huston movie!* Fat City *(from what I read) is about itinerant farm workers who go into the boxing ring for money and glory and come out with "more pain and emptiness."*
>
> *Huston tried to pep up the movie with things that weren't in the script because the story was so low-key. The first thing he did when he saw the script was to rewrite it, so the author did too, six*

*or seven times, in order to save his story, and the final script is*
*close to the original novel.*

*Huston is described as "baggy-eyed, seamy-faced, a large man*
*gone heavy around the middle, seemingly more interested in his*
*cigar than the movie he was making."*

*It sounds like Huston does whatever he wants to with film-*
*scripts. In this book, a fight is finally won by one boxer outlasting*
*the other. Huston changes it, making it very active with even a*
*knockdown. The author goes out of his mind. He says at one*
*point, "The movie winds up being both cruder and simpler than*
*the book. Somehow the irony is gone." (Leonard Gardner is the*
*author.)*

*The ending of this article reminded me very much of* The Red
Badge of Courage. *The author of the article, Leonard Shecter,*
*says, "Movies are, after all, made in the cutting room, a place*
*where no writer can function. Too dark."*

In that class we all knew a lot about John Huston from reading *Picture.* Students had debated him: some hated him for his arrogance;
others praised him as individual and creative. We were all hungry for
more about him, and Diane Vint had sensed that. She chose some
pointed things about him out of the *Look* magazine article and gave
them to us. In a widely ranging course like this one, which included
consideration of newspapers, magazines, film, television, still pictures,
and radio—such additive comment is essential to hold things together.
Freed of the pressure of grades, of appearing to help the teacher out
only to improve their grades, my students were beginning to add to the
stream of materials we were considering in that class. In doing this
they were balancing the other thrust of the class, which was to encourage each student to investigate matters that interested him as an individual with his own set of past experiences and predilections.

From my earlier failure in the Senior Seminar, I had learned to
offset the scattering effect of individual interests. I assigned everyone
one book to read. I showed everyone several films. I had everyone
study one magazine and one or two newspapers. At the same time the
students were free to write journal entries about any mass communications that struck them anywhere at any time.

☐

I hadn't expected the journal entries would be so useful. Mainly I
was trying to teach students how to produce perceptive criticisms of
the mass media. I wanted written comments that could be responded to
by their classmates—a test that counts. But if a student departed from
a communication and began discussing something else related to it, I
was able to exhibit to the class his insights about other things than

mass communications. Why not? The subject of study in the university is man and how he and his environment act upon each other. As long as a student is commenting perceptively on that subject, his remarks cannot be irrelevant to any course taught there. When he becomes gassy or obvious or incomprehensible, then he may be said to be "off the subject." With all that freedom, seldom did the students in that mass media course waste our time. Rather,

> *The film we saw yesterday in class,* High School, *was what a future teacher might describe as a rude awakening—not because we do not know what the situation is in a typical classroom but simply because as I grow nearer to graduating I realize more and more how very unequipped I am to handle the situation. As anyone who watched the film realized, high school is a most important part of one's life, and to stifle the students as this film so well depicted without even realizing it, as many of the teachers did not, is the saddest part of the whole situation. Why do people become so routinized and set in their own ways that they cannot see clearly? I suppose I do know why—it is too much trouble and effort to keep an open mind and always be searching for answers. Routine methods are less work, less thoughts, and fewer head-aches. Oh, how I hope I have headaches!*
>
> *Watching the movie recalled to my mind as probably to every-one else's in the class my high school days. Some of the film was boring for I knew exactly what was going to happen, perhaps sometimes even word for word. Counselors who knew nothing really about colleges and requirements and your ability tried to steer you into a Catholic all-girl school if they thought you were sweet and innocent, or a strict academic school with no social functions if you were intelligent, or a marriage if you were pres-ently interested in home economics. The counselors in the film were so typical it scared me. I suppose they were themselves, as even the other teachers and administrators in the school, because they felt they were a "model school." ... How do you deal with that complete boredom for eight hours a day, five days a week—wanting to please them, to stimulate them, to get them interested? A relatively age-old question—I don't think so—because I don't think the main body of teachers cares, at least the established ones. Teaching is a job—to cover one chap-ter a week from pp. 95-130, two homework sheets to be handed in and a quiz at the end of the week to check memorization. The only thing fresh teachers have going for them is their attitude, I hope, perhaps caring more about the individual than the subject matter. A greater difficulty they face than established teachers though is the anxiety to try to change and rearrange what established teachers possess—and that is their power to keep things running smoothly for themselves. Stimulating and fresh*

*ideas—mine are few but what little I do have going for me I intend to use. Established math teacher—I hope not. That rut I don't need.*

Rereading this entry as I write this book, I was struck by the similarity between the student's observation:

*. . . established teachers possess . . . power to keep things running smoothly for themselves.*

and Leo Tolstoy's comment:

The teacher always involuntarily strives after selecting that method of instruction which is most convenient for himself. [*Tolstoy on Education* (Chicago: University of Chicago Press, 1967), p. 264.]

As a teacher of writing, I had a hard time refraining from commenting on the awkwardness in my student's journal entry, but I refrained. Few students who care about what they are saying speak in such a strained voice as this writer did. If I had tried to influence my students' writing style by enunciating a "requirement," they would have been right back in that high school the film depicted—stiff, tongue-tied.

☐

Years ago I remember reading in the catalog of the university where I taught that hopefully in four years the student would learn habits of "independent thinking." Maybe a few, I thought, but I was glad for the word "hopefully." Now I am shaken to realize that many of my students come to me with this capability—if I can only free them from counter habits learned in school, often from teachers the likes of me in my first seventeen years, and sometimes me right now. The writer of the following entry, Kate Mack, immediately showed me she had an independent mind, by looking hard at a film that had been widely and extravagantly praised long before she saw it.

*I saw 2001: A Space Odyssey the other day—mostly because everyone told me how great it was, but also because it was ladies day and I could get in cheap.*

   *When I got to the theatre it was five minutes after the movie had started; a man was at the ticket booth with a handful of tickets—he was getting 100. Every time the lady sent five more tickets out the slot, the machine jammed and the tickets had rips down the center. After each mutilated five came out, she tried to fix the machine and several times asked how many he already had, and he proceeded to count all the tickets in his hand again and insist again that if she would just let him get a hold on the first ticket coming out, he could pull the rest out. Each of them glanced at me three or four times while this was going on but neither said anything or offered to sell me one lousy ticket before the movie ended and Christmas came. I watched this comedy for more than five minutes before I was annoyed enough to walk in without a ticket. I would explain to the ticket ripper that I didn't want to miss the movie waiting to buy the ticket. As soon as I got inside I realized that the man outside was supposed to be inside taking tickets. Oops. What do you know, I'm on the other side of THE MAN and I haven't spent a penny. I didn't want it to seem like I sneaked in (well, I didn't . . . really. I didn't rush back out to pay either, though); so I talked to the popcorn girl and bought a fudgesicle and then went into the movie. On the screen some men were having a very serious meeting, getting ready for something.*

*For a long time I was lost trying to figure out what was going on, but gradually—after meeting the astronauts and Hal the robot—things began to make more sense (not a lot of sense, but more sense). A mission to Venus [Jupiter] to find out about signals from that planet, two astronauts awake and functioning on the ship while all the rest of the crew hibernated in boxes until needed, and Hal in charge of everything crucial—these points were all made clear to the viewer before the doubt about Hal seeped into the story. I thought Hal was neat, in a spooky way—a talking machine that (who?) knew everything, controlled almost everything, and after his initial mistake or miscalculation, acted more like a human than a machine, and really fouled things up. Hal predicted that something would go wrong with a certain piece of the spaceship within seventy-two hours so the astronauts examined it and the scientists back home examined it, but nothing was found wrong. They all decided to put the piece back and let it function until it failed and then diagnose and fix the problem.*

*But Hal had made a mistake. His prediction was wrong, there was nothing the matter with the machinery. The astronauts wondered if Hal could be the first computer of his series to err, and decided that he might have to be disconnected. Although the astronauts tried to keep their conversation from Hal, he was able to read their lips and understand their doubts about him. From then on, Hal acted very defensively and more things began to go wrong. The rest of the crew died in their boxes and when Dave went out to put the "faulty" piece where it belonged, Hal didn't open the door to let him back in and Dave was left floating in space. Dan, the only astronaut left, climbed up to Hal's memory bank and disconnected everything while Hal pleaded with him and confessed to making mistakes, and promised to do better and*

*even admitted he was afraid (rather unusual for a machine!).
Dan finished the job, though, and finished Hal. The spacecraft
continued on its way with only Dan conscious, and the rest of the
movie is either a fantastic dream of Dan's before he dies or an
account of Dan's perception of the entry into the atmosphere of
Venus with flashing, swirling colors, and shows us the end of his
life as an old man and as a still older man in bed with the symbolic monolith still present. Since I missed the first part of the
movie, I didn't immediately understand the full meaning or feel
the impact of this big black thing that seemed to follow man
through time and consciousness, but the embryo at the end gave
me a strong inkling. When the lights came back on, I sat there for
thirty seconds and felt disappointed in the movie. I'm not sure
why exactly. The movie didn't hang together; there were a lot of
unexplained things, and for some reason the whole movie seemed
fake and phony to me. Maybe it's all my fault—for entering the
theatre expecting to see a "great" movie (maybe great movies are
always unexpected) and for free, yet. Serves me right, right?
That's one movie I'm glad I didn't have to pay to see.*

☐

In this book I furnish the reader lively examples of my students'
work. I do not mean to imply that everything written in the mass-
media journals was fresh and thoughtful. I suppose sixty percent of
what I read was dull or mediocre. By far the longest entry I received
was a pointless, interminable report of a trip to a big city museum
taken by a college class, with paragraph after paragraph of unrelated
description of the appearance and behavior of the students in the bus,
of the categories of paintings seen in the museum, all sinking at the
end into a romantic sunset. Several members of the class said they
found the report boring and insignificant—quite the most adverse criticism of a student work in the whole semester—but the writer remained
convinced she had written an epic travel story.

☐

When I asked the students in this class to become newspaper
reporters (in the assignment I mentioned earlier, the one that had
always failed), they did the job unprofessionally, often with ridiculous,
laughable incompetence. But they did it, and they were not loath to
discuss the difference between their work and that of professionals.
They did not feel injured or insulted. They were not being graded.
Before we were through discussing those reports (they were given two
reporting assignments), we had discussed in class almost every
difficulty in reporting, from when to repeat a word or use an abbrevia-
tion to whether to suppress a story in the interests of public safety.

A student from Africa wrote a report of his conversations with persons in a suburb of our city who were arming themselves to suppress Blacks, who they supposed were ready to move forcefully into their neighborhood. An older woman who lived in that suburb said she had no knowledge or suspicion that such persons were her neighbors. We talked about the difficulty of getting verifiable facts in such reporting, of quoting without risking libel suits, of creating false fears on the basis of rumor. I debated with myself, and then with the class, whether we should pass these secondhand reports of vigilantes to community officials or to the local newspaper. I decided against it, and have since heard no reports of armed violence in that suburb. But the question became real for all of us, and we began to understand the complexity of being objective and responsible as a newspaperman.

☐

Each point about news reporting that came up in that class arose from accounts the students had written. One girl wrote this statement:

> *Two girls on two horses closely followed by two dogs canter around the Michigan hay field. A boy on a tractor, dragging the mower, is circling, cutting hay. Gradually the patch of tall hay shrinks as the tractor chugs around another corner and another strip of hay falls flat.*
>
> *Now as the horses circle the outer edge of the field and the tractor around the inside, the dogs run helter-skelter, sniffing at this, chasing that, and running for the joy of running, tongues flapping.*
>
> *Suddenly a shriek. The horses stop, the girls look. Amiga, the small black dog, screams away from the tractor toward the horses, one front leg dangling. The girls stare. The smaller girl screams and cries, "Amiga! Miga, Miga. . . ." Both girls leap down and run toward the whimpering dog. Her leg is off, hanging only by a piece of skin. Blood shoots out rhythmically. . . .*
>
> *NOTE: Phooey—this is not appropriate for a newspaper article, really, and might not even be appropriate for a journal entry. It's just that I was so deeply moved by the incident.*

That started out to be a newspaper report, but the writer thought better. I knew she didn't want me to present it to class, but I did anyway, without naming her. The little story served as a test case: What is news, anyway? The class talked about the question. Ordinarily newspapers do not cover the death of a dog or cat. One student said she had noticed that few news stories ever listed dogs or cats as victims in car crashes that "killed all the occupants." Why not? Was not the dog a valued member of the family? Was the death of Amiga, here told dramatically and poignantly, not more significant than that day's officially sanctioned news that Elizabeth Taylor had received a necklace costing thousands of dollars?

And the style of the story. The girls were not identified, their address not given. The whole piece has more the sound of a poem or short story than a news report. Why do news stories contain such factual information? When do they need to be more or less factual? Some of these questions were mine, some were the students'. But they all arose from something a student had done.

In this class we were constantly trying to answer these questions to the satisfaction of everyone in the room, as this or that student's report forced us to. I like to talk about precisely those problems with newsmen. To stretch them to think of the function of a newspaper. The question that had occupied me in my doctoral thesis—"How much subjectivity should a reporter show in newspaper writing?"—we dealt with in that class again and again, and it came up naturally, without my having to force discussion. A naive story about an accident to a student's dog led to the profoundest questions about the mass media.

I have learned to make the students' thought and experience one of the points supporting the axis of my teaching. The other point is the authoritative knowledge of the course, including my own, that existed before those students entered the room. In studying the constitution and needs of human beings we have always right with us in the room that constitution and those needs. For the students and I are people, the proper subject of all scholastic attention, along with the physical environment we inhabit.

☐

In that class the students were working with their stuff as well as the teacher's. But it became mine soon, and I could extend their vision. At what was often the right moment I could introduce some of my experience or expertise. In the past I had been cramming it in their ears day after day and they had rejected it. Now they were habitually recording honest responses to communications they had encountered. They were not being wary or coy. They did not have to appear stupid while hesiating to give an opinion that might not agree with mine. A student wrote in his journal:

> *I recently took my fiancée to see* Big Jake, *starring John Wayne and Richard Boone. Jenny didn't like the sickening part. She got mad at me and thought I was some kind of blood-hungry fiend. She just cannot stand the sight of blood and human suffering. She gets upset at me because we always seem to go to more good guy, bad guy, shoot 'em up westerns than we do to Ali McGraw and Ryan O'Neal type flicks.*
>
> *From the start of the movie all the way through I was very concerned about the physical well being of my arm. During any*

*action she would take out her aggression on my left arm. All the hate she had for the bad guys when they were brawling with Duke and his boys was released on my arm.*

*Jenny lives the movie, she becomes a real member of the show. She can feel the joy, sorrow, and pain that the movie depicts. At the end of the movie a marginal hero dies, gets butchered up very badly along with Duke's dog. She blamed me for letting them die. I never laughed so much. I told her I was sorry and if she wanted to sit through it again I'd promise her that they wouldn't die. That tickled her and everything was all right except for my damn arm.*

At the same time, as so often happened in that class, another student wrote on John Wayne in his journal. I cannot find a copy of his comments. It was a deep analysis of how falseness and corruption are wedded in John Wayne's screen characters. The Nazi streak in the whole business—the smiling, blustering killer or ruffian and the warm-hearted adulation of him from the audience.

When I brought these two entries before the class we had the stuff for a discussion of violence in the media, of the formula story ("good guys, bad guys," as my student had said), of the whole difficult matter of entertainment versus truth. I hate John Wayne, his movies, and everything about him. But I used to like Jackie Gleason's formula TV show *The Honeymooners,* with Art Carney. What differences between the formulas? What about patterns in communication? In this class I was able to make distinctions about such things with more ease and force than ever before. And so were the students. They were split in opinion, so I was not coming on as the supreme voice, which speaks in the test and arouses fear in every student that he may suffer if his honest opinion does not agree with the teacher's. In this class there was no compulsion for students to accept my judgments. I presented them, not as the lengthy and boring opinions I used to deliver; these were all the more attractive and persuasive because they arose out of the materials the students were furnishing.

I was surprised to find students frequently bringing to class apposite materials—reviews of a film someone had mentioned in his journal, a background article on a documentary director we had discussed. And they were always penetrating and relevant. Because of the construction of the class the students were freed from desires to toady. Doing away with grades had done away with flattery, whose poisonous effect the flattered seldom recognize.

One day in the student newspaper I noticed a review of a film a student had discussed in his journal. I picked up enough copies of the paper for the whole class and we discussed it, some arguing with our student writer that the campus critic was totally destructive and others siding with him. At the next meeting a girl brought a review of the same film by Stanley Kauffmann, *The New Republic*'s experienced and intellectual critic. It was long and gave us a chance to see what could be done with more space and more critical experience. I could not have furnished so many timely professional additions to the course as these students provided. I am only one person, busy, limited. As we went along we were building our relevant and contemporary textbooks for the course. More than half of it consisted of writing by my students.

☐

The course was loosely constructed, but nothing like that mad Senior Seminar I described earlier. I knew what I wanted to stress. I was open to new possibilities that might come up in the students' journals. Probably one of the reasons the course went so well was that I had studied the mass media for over twenty years and had unsuccessfully taught courses about them for almost the same stretch of time. I say "one of the reasons" because I want to link those seeming opposites: I was learned and not yet arrogant, a difficult and rare condition for a teacher.

I will not here say much about the principles and realities I wanted the students to face, but I must say a little so that the reader does not believe the course was undirected. Like Lucius Garvin, I wanted these students, who had seldom thought systematically about my subject, to encounter a man who had. Slowly, and when the occasion seemed right, I brought up these notions as criteria for judging communications: (1) Truth to life. That includes the truth to life in an imagined work like *Alice in Wonderland* or *The Wizard of Oz;* (2) Surprise. That which arises naturally and validly out of circumstances and that which is forced upon circumstances for the sake of sensation; (3) the pattern of *repeat and vary*, when it leads to strength and when to cliché and stock response.

As one or another journal entry snagged us in controversy, I slowly tried to turn the class toward analyzing the nature of perception, the function of the observer's past experience as well as the function of the thing he is observing. In a small way I introduced the subject of the nature of communication by pictures.

☐

Two-thirds of the way through the course I realized that I was introducing these students to many essentials about communication in such an unpressured situation that they emerged as essentials rather than prescribed items for the next test. There were no tests as such, but much testing of our ideas.

When I asked the students to look at magazines of their choice and comment on specific aspects of them, I knew that the number of subscribers a magazine possesses has an effect on what it will try to be.

In the past I have asked each student to go to the library and look up in *Ayer's Directory of Publications* the circulation of the magazine they were examining and reporting on. I had arranged that the project be exhaustive. Each student presented a twenty-minute report, touching upon aspects of communication I had named, and adding his own observations. It was a dreadful stratagem on my part. We become tired of listening to the reports. Many seemed to echo others, except for different names.

Now I simply ask students to comment on things in magazines that interest them, and I choose what I consider the most valuable comments and present them dittoed before the class. Always I open that process by saying that anyone who has a comment he would like the class to respond to will be given that opportunity. Soon we have hit all the points that used to come up in the exhaustive method, and few are bored.

In this class I suddenly wondered why I should send all the students to one reference book when one student could get a representative list of circulation figures for the whole class. I asked for a volunteer, paid her twenty-five cents (meant to make it fifty, but didn't have any more change on me, and later made good), and Kate Mack said smiling, "Sure, I have to go to the library today anyhow." She was absent on the following day, but sent the figures with another student. They were perfect. It was a shorter list than I would have made, and better. Just long enough to hold the interest of the class, it included figures for all the magazines that had been discussed so far in class and a sampling of other representatives ones, including figures for *Time* magazine showing a breakdown for foreign editions, which gave me the opportunity to say something about the Mexican edition of *Time* which I had been reading during the past year.

I know how stupid this anecdote makes me seem. I am that stupid, a professor trained in the time-honored educational system of the U.S. I have been conditioned to seeing all the students in a class do one thing: carry out an assignment which gives me what I ask for—not something I need, not something they need, not something that would be useful to them as a group or as individuals going somewhere both they and I would like them to go. I am a professional interested in mass media. So when I look at communications I want to cover them thoroughly, and later perhaps select from my full data what will be useful for my purposes. My bent is to require students to do the same. But they are taking a general course, not majoring in this subject. Frequently their enthusiasm lies elsewhere. When I give them a chance to work on their own, without specific assignment, they do not overkill the subject. My job is to arrange the course so that we penetrate deeply at times, not try to cover widely. I am learning.

□

Often I was disappointed that many students did not push far enough in their comments on communications. When I received a complex and subtle analysis, I always reproduced it for the class, thinking its example would lead all the others to see the thinness of some of their efforts. Several students rarely produced valuable journal entries. They were satisfied with a bare judgment that did not take them into the whole communication situation. Frequently when their comments were attacked by other students, they probed deeper.

I am learning to consider what my students can do with their knowledge. I am not interested in their simple ability to reproduce my knowledge upon command. When one member of this mass-media class missed several early meetings and made this journal entry on newspapers, I was led to remember how empty are most student papers in college.

*Newspaper—an important source of news. Probably the second largest (TV being number 1) way of informing a great number of people of important events taking place all over the world and recently out of this world. The newspaper can be a form of amusement, the comic section, and can also let people know where to go for entertainment. People buy and sell things through the paper. It helps people find jobs. Advertisement is a big part of every paper. This not only helps pay for the cost of the newspaper but also benefits the reader by telling him where to go for "special sales" on certain items. Through columns like Ann Landers, people can write in about personal problems. I think the newspaper is an important social invention of man. A drawback of the paper is that they tend to be biased. Most of the important decisions as to what goes into print are made by a comparatively small group of men.*

An incredible recital of nothings. I remembered when my teaching used to elicit dozens of such papers about "important" things the student thought I thought were important. This boy wasn't there when Amiga's leg was shorn off in the hay field. I branded him imbecile. Later in the course, when he saw what other students were doing, he came up with some original opinions.

□

Every teacher faces the difficulty of judging how his students are doing, even when he has before him the evidence of original thought. Does he admire it because it comes from his student? Or from a student who has done poorly in the past? Or is the work genuinely significant? I like the following journal entry because it shows the ability to appreciate a talent in someone the judge generally dislikes, and it brings to bear personal experience upon a judgment of a public act with the kind of leap implicit in every good metaphor. Therefore I suspect my judgment of it is valid although another reader may not like it so much as I do.

*A couple of nights ago I watched Johnny Carson for the first time in five months. ... The show begins with that typical Carson entrance, all smiles and happiness. The monologue begins and Carson talks about the same things—articles in newspapers, double-entendre jokes, or the clothes of Doc. If the monologue is failing (as it was this night), Carson will go into his bad "monologue routine"—"So that's how you treat an old War Vet," or he will say, "Laugh or get out" or something like this. Finally Carson will do his golf stroke and the monologue is over.*

*After an endless series of commercials, Carson returns. For a couple of minutes he and McMahon will talk, asking one another how the other feels and also plugging one another. "Well, Ed, speaking of money, I'll be in Las Vegas next week—" Then Ed will start talking about all his charitable organizations or his latest diet. ...*

*While watching Carson I noticed the blatant phoniness of the show. It reminded me of the characters in* Picture *and their Hollywood facade of friendliness. Of course, it's Carson's job to be cheerful and jolly every night but I find it hard to accept. He is a human being and has his bad times like all of us do. ... But I still sympathize with Carson. In fact, I have a vague idea of how he feels. When I hitchhiked across country with two of my friends, we understood our obligation to carry on a conversation with the person that picked us up. So we would take turns initiating conversations and keeping them going. Many times this would be simple because the driver would be an interesting person to talk to. But at other times I would have to rack my brain for decent questions to ask the driver so we could continue our conversation. Also you have to have tact, patience, and a certain amount of understanding so the conversation will be pleasant. It's hard work and many times I wished I was sleeping in the back seat instead of sitting up front rapping with the driver.*

I thought this entry had ended with an insight. When I read it to the class my supposition was confirmed. There were mutterings of "Yeah," and "That's right. I've done that, too." The task of judging students is both eased and made surer when a teacher uses the seminar method.

☐

In General Education courses Humanities teachers are trying to induce students to like Aeschylus and Beethoven and Picasso, whom they like, or think they like. In Criticism of Mass Media I am trying to induce my students to appreciate *The New York Times* and *The New Republic* more than *The Chicago Tribune* and *Mad* Magazine. Or *The Mary Tyler Moore Show* more than *Dragnet*. All teachers are trying to give students standards that will enrich their lives. I have found I can't do it by lecturing. I can't do it by showing students what I like and saying it's the best. Rather I must give them the chance to build their own standards while confronting mine and those of other students. I must give myself the chance to see their own standards appear in a natural way—with the basis for them evident to everyone. Above all, I must not test them for their knowledge of and acceptance of my standards. They know when that is happening, and they react. Either they refuse to look or think, or they begin fawning upon me.

Without grades the teacher's voice still carries the weight of his position. The class begins when he arrives. He is at the least a chairperson. The students have paid to meet with him. Nothing is easier for him than to talk about opening the minds of students while he closes the classroom off from opinions and standards other than his own.

☐

I have said this course was loosely run. Since many Free Schoolers may consider my notions of freedom constrained, I will specify further some of the kinds of freedom and discipline that characterized this class.

I made sure that all students participated in a few common activities so they could see their judgment operating on the same materials. I introduced the study of film by requiring every student to read Lillian Ross's *Picture*. This is a lively, intimately revealing book first published in *The New Yorker*. The method of studying it was standard: read and record in the journal any strong reaction you had to any part or aspect of the book. We took two weeks to read it and react. Because it presented so many matters human, technical, artistic, financial, it became a key reference for subsequent discussions. For example, the entry I have quoted on the Johnny Carson show alluded to *Picture* in a way that everyone in the class understood. It is this practice which teachers complain their students never engage in—using their knowledge, building on it, making their reading and inquiry pay off.

In such a broad course the technicalities of each medium could not be studied thoroughly. But the students were writing almost every day. Lillian Ross was writing. Students were reading copies of *The New York Times* and *The Village Voice* which I had passed out to them. They had all bought two issues of *TV Guide*. So we could talk a little about what made good writing, how an editor and a writer tightened up his work, what sorts of words fit what sorts of audience, etc. We had writers and readers available and could study what they did.

In a limited way we could also study the use of television cameras. One day an older woman turned in a journal that included this entry:

> *I am amazed at the close-up a TV viewer gets of football players. When the team is in a huddle the cameras get right up there and have a close-up of a particular player. And then when the ball goes on its journey, whether it be by air or by ground, the camera follows it better than I can when I'm at the game. They can switch from a long view to a close-up and back again in seconds.*
>
> *And the replays. If a guy happens to be downfield for a pass and the quarterback never gets the ball out of his hands, the camera is showing the quarterback. But they can also replay the guy downfield being tackled.*
>
> *Sunday I watched the Green Bay Packers play the Lions. A Detroit player was eliminated from the game for poor sportsmanship. He left the field and nothing more was said. Then about ten minutes later the camera got a closeup of him way over in the far corner behind the dugout wall, still watching the game. The cameras seem to be able to get everywhere on the field. Even a bird's-eye view of the field can be flashed on the TV screen to show a band formation. I am really (that word again) amazed. I would love to be near a TV camera to see how they can complete all those tasks.*

Several days later a student said, "Down there in the courtyard there's a guy with a little TV camera." I looked. Another student reported that the camera and a monitor were being kept out there all day and anyone who wanted to use the camera or see how he looked on TV could do so. I escorted the whole class down there at once. We spent a half hour in the courtyard playing around with one of the essential instruments of our study. A week later I took the class to the university TV studio where the manager, a brilliant young man who wants more to introduce students to the potentialities of TV than to protect his equipment, let the students play around with his sophisticated, expensive equipment. A few rules: don't blow out the camera by pointing it at the floodlights, don't try to turn the camera when it's in lock position.

I had asked the manager to let the students play with the equipment first, then to explain the facilities later. He did this. For a few minutes persons brave enough operated the cameras and appeared before them. When they got tired, about six students spontaneously put on a show of their own, one sitting at a piano, another emceeing an interview program. I stood there marveling at their nerve. In college days I would have hidden in a far corner.

After we had a good look at the equipment, including the engineering room, the manager talked briefly about the future of television when cable TV would furnish so many channels that the medium could be used as a genuine learning and teaching device with which a person could study his own performances. The class ate those two hours as if they were ice-cream cones.

☐

One of my teacher friends had arranged to show Frederic Wiseman's searing documentary *High School*—a real institution in America photographed as if by a hidden camera. This film represented a level of shocking truth against which we could measure many TV shows and films that students commented on in journals. But again the discussion was open; some students saw the dangers inherent in showing truths about school in contrast to the bland pictures on education commonly available from the Audio Visual Department. We got into matters of objectivity and truth again, and I think everyone saw that there is no neat formula for reporting by word or picture.

☐

The ongoing act in that class was the students writing in journals. Sometimes I dictated that they should write about one subject—like the book *Picture.* Usually I simply said write about a mass communication that has struck you hard. After we saw *High School* a few students wrote about it, but not all. Occasionally this random writing produced half a dozen entries on the same communication and we could compare responses. Often every student wrote on his own subject and faced the difficulty of communicating a judgment about something the others had not seen or heard.

In setting up the journal keeping I had said at the outset that I expected most of the entries to criticize mass communications, but if a student felt like recording something else in his journal he was free to do so. Several students from time to time presented striking observations of society or a piece of their own life that did not directly touch mass communication. Several were so lively that I dittoed them with the other entries for presentation to the class.

Class discussion disappointed me a little because about a third of the group said little all semester long. I have yet to find ways of loosening the tongues of all the students in any of my classes. A few wrote relatively little in their journals and I prodded two or three. Generally in all my classes I am able to get more regular writing out of students than regular talking. I made one slip at the third meeting of class. A girl who had come on strong in discussion and shown her classmates that it was possible to talk intelligently off the cuff had dominated both the first and second sessions. I had determined, as is my policy, to let her know the dangers involved. If she talked too much, no matter how brilliantly, she would lose the element of surprise and novelty, perhaps eventually her audience. She had come up after class to say something to me and I began to tell her about talking too much when another student and then another approached us. I thought maybe I should stop and take her out in the hall for privacy, but since I had already begun my remarks, I continued. She was shocked and suddenly silent. After that she began cutting class frequently, and for the last half of the semester appeared only a few times. She proved one of the most prejudiced writers in the class. She needed to put her opinions up against others in the classroom and learn to judge after she knew something. I think she was committed to what students call the Movement and could have profited from older students who in their journal entries had talked about both the virtues and dangers of condemning everything about American institutions. But my quick word had cut her off. Perhaps there were other reasons she dropped out, but I know my action was one of the causes.

☐

At the end of the course I asked the students to turn in their grades and written statements of why they had arrived at them. I also gave them the option of having me grade them. No one took that option. I returned to my office that day with their comments, curious. I was sure most of these decent young persons would give themselves a "B" and that would be all right with me. I think I would have given them these grades:

$$A - 6$$
$$B - 15$$
$$C - 5$$
$$D - 2$$

When I recorded what the students had given themselves it looked like this:

$$A - 22$$
$$B - 4$$
$$C - 1$$

The girl whom I had shut up was not present to grade herself, so I gave her a "D."

I was outraged. Two students whose journal entries had been of no help to their fellow students had given themselves "A." I was sure they must have seen that the long and complex and surprising entries by some of their classmates had educated us all, while theirs had usually pointed out the obvious, and then without vitality. But no, they found reasons, many of them bad, I thought, for taking "A." Here are excerpts from a few of the substantiations for grading.

1. *I've got an all "A" semester going and I don't want this class to spoil it.*

2. *I've written a lot. Not just what you wanted—but I did hand in the assignments. I've become more aware of the ambiguity of the news—the bias—the power of a journalist or reporter and the difficulty of his job.*

3. *You said that you were pressing for academic freedom in this class without the worry of grades hanging over our heads. I took you at your word and decided from the first day of class I would receive a four-hour "A" from a general studies class that I chose only for the reason that it was required and it fit my time slot.*

4. *I got a lot out of the class pertaining to movies, TV production and watching. I wasn't producing for you but for myself, and through discussions about things I picked up in class, with others, I got even more. I feel you should get an "A" for the way you taught the class so I feel I deserve an "A" for what I got out of it.*

5. *Particularly because I need to keep the Grade Point Average up for financial reasons, I would grade myself—"A."*

6. *I have found this course to be very interesting and it has helped me to open my eyes and look into different communications to see what is really* [that word again!] *being said. I have enjoyed the different assignments, especially the ones dealing with movies and the book* Picture. *I learned more from that book than what I thought I would. My assignments have always been complete, on time, and handed in on schedule. Also my attendance has been regular—I've only missed one class. I feel that I have done just as much work as anyone else in the class. . . .*

Those who had done the weakest work and misjudged their performance wrote much of their defense in Engfish sentences. Comments by other students were much more forcefully stated.

One student whom I would have given an "A" gave himself a "B." My reaction to this grading may amuse a reader who knows I believe grades are imprecise and usually harmful to learning. Ordinarily I have a clear idea of a few students I think deserve "A" in a course and a few who did badly, deserving perhaps "C" or "D." But there are dozens of decisons I have to make every semester that I am not sure of. "B" or "A"? "C" or "B"? The only grades that would have made sense to me in that class were "Pass" and "Fail." I was angry with students who took "A" but had never educated the rest of us in that room. My standard was finally nothing quantitative and not a response to how much had been memorized and given back to the teacher. I think the students undermined the grading system; but I cannot condemn them, for I agree that it is a farce.

I give more weight than usual to the contention by many students that they learned more than their journals or class comments showed, for both powerful and weak students made that remark. In that class they found that a mass communication can arouse highly different responses in attentive, intelligent persons. They were not watching just the usual conflict between a "rebellious" student and a dominating teacher.

I am pleased with that class. I must now learn to introduce more rigor; to elicit more and better journal entries and class discussion. But I know the course succeeded. Without tests and punative grades I was able to bring more minds than ever before seriously and often enjoyably to bear upon the complexities of the mass media.

## Chapter 8
# Sea of Black

☐

The white man's brains that today explore space should have told the slavemaster that any slave, if he is educated, will no longer fear his master. History shows that an educated slave always begins to ask, and next demand, equality with his master.

Malcolm X, *The Autobiography of Malcolm X*
(New York: Grove Press, 1965), p. 268.

☐

One September I stood waiting down the hall from my freshman writing classroom. I saw several Blacks enter the room. Good. Ordinarily I have no more than one or two in a class. When I looked again, there were more. At four minutes past the hour I walked through the door and found thirteen Blacks and five Whites.

I smiled and said a few words. Stony response. The eyes up, daring me to prove a honky could do something not insulting or repressive. I know that suggests I saw only the eyes of Blacks. They were all I saw.

I was ready—as I have often been these days—for an unfriendly Black response. Ready, but suffering under those stares. What should I do? I was not going to begin with some damnfool defensive sugarcoated promise of love. I talked about the course.

My initial task in any class is to convince students they must, for perhaps the first time in school, speak and write honestly. How could I—standing in front of centuries of my tribe's lies—ask that of thirteen Blacks? I wanted to demonstrate instantly I was going to be fair. Telling them would be no good. I took a risk. I had brought a copy of a magazine of student writing published by a high-school teacher and me. From it I read a black student's paper on being in love with a white girl. He had interspersed remarks by Eldridge Cleaver and others about the black man's hangup on white women with his own story of falling in love. I read along, my voice quavering. Maybe too bold for the first day? As I read, I looked up occasionally. Stone. From everyone. But they were listening. When I finished I hoped for spontaneous mutters or cries of approval, as I had heard in the past for this account. I said the paper represented research that for a change meant something to the writer. No response.

☐

Then I told the people before me to find a quiet place, write down whatever came into their heads as fast as they could, without thinking of punctuation or other mechanics—twice, for fifteen minutes each time. Bring the papers to the next class.

The first free writings were as good as I get from any freshmen. In all but two papers I could find a paragraph competently and honestly written. One about a motorcycle accident seemed curiously amoral.

*They said I hit her but I'm almost positive I missed, but I still can hear her scream when she came in the light of my cycle ... I'm glad she wasn't hurt too bad, she's okay and everything but we both won't forget it. Now I got a bigger bike and am driving wilder than ever. I guess maybe because I got the power to scoot along better, but it still scares me to see kids on bikes when I'm driving anything.*

The writer was white.

More than half of the black students touched upon black-white relationships. Here's one paper:

*Sitting here in my room. There are four girls in here. Two are white. Two are black. The white girls say they are our friends, but I wonder if they really feel if we are as much as they are, if they consider us as people. Now I think if I really consider them as people. I wonder what the majority of white people really think of me. Because my skin is black why I'm considered as a destroyer and hateful person. I'm falling in a ditch and the two white so-called girl friends are standing there with their white buddies. But they don't try to help me. I'm falling. I need help. But they just let me fall in the ditch.*

*I wonder why are Blacks turning against Blacks and Whites are turning against Whites. Now everyone's turning against everyone. Now I'm looking down a hill and the whole damn nation is falling down. Finally the damn nation falls down and we're all dead because we all can't live together and for each other.*

Another:

*My roommate is a very selfish, unconcerned, and nasty person. She doesn't know how to share a room with someone and doesn't try. She wants everything to go her way and nothing yours. She dislikes every thing that I like. She decorated the room to her taste to satisfy her but not the both of us. She has a guitar that she plays that doesn't sound so hot. She throws her clothes and other items around the room when I keep mine together. She brings all types of people to the room whether I'm asleep or not and when I have company it really bothers her. She leaves the door open when I like privacy. I'm a quiet person and she is loud. I enjoy people a lot and try to get along with everyone but with her it is difficult. Is it because she's white and I'm black?*

I read aloud papers against Whites with no comment. The five white students said nothing. Occasionally a Black spoke, but no extended discussion. I talked about what was good in the writing and invited comments. I got few but knew from past experience that we were off to a fine start. Most of the Blacks were writing honestly and in a class run by a white man. I was not reading Engfish.

My method would work perfectly for black students because it did not try to standardize students' language.

But the writing got worse. Much of it was dull. It lost the echoes of sermons and street talk and it almost never said enough. In an assigned twenty minutes, several black girls turned out no more than this, for example:

> *While laying here thinking over things my family and I use to do.*
> *It wasn't easy for me to say good-bye to them. All I could say was so-long for now.*
> *My parents aren't like some parents that keep their little girls at home and don't give them freedom, they were the type that gave me what I which* [wish] *if they could give. Like some girls that have parents that won't give them freedom when they get away they are on the wild.*

The writing stopped there.

I began to feel uncomfortable going to that class. Usually I received only one or two writings likely to call forth admiration from the group. Even the good ones elicited little praise. We had all fallen in the ditch.

One day a black student who had been writing more fully than the others, albeit tamely, about his experiences in sports, said, "Is this all we're going to do? Read papers every day and talk about them?"

"That's what the course is going to be," I had to say. "It's a seminar. Every week you should be writing ever longer and more complex papers, and soon we'll be discussing fine points of writing."

A girl said, "How about grammar? Are we just going to talk about whether we like something we wrote? I think we need some punctuation and spelling and things like that to get through college."

I was sinking. My writing classes never before had touched so low early in the semester. I told the girl that first a person has to write something valuable to himself and others before work on the mechanics of writing will pay off. Later, at the time for reading work for publication, we would sharpen and polish.

About four weeks into the class, two of the young white men turned in papers that impressed the group. Then Melissa Cooper wrote this one:

> *He drove up in a '69 Electra and smiled when he saw someone standing in the door anticipating his arrival.*
> *"For a minute there you looked exactly like your mother," he said with a pleasant voice. "Is she home?"*
> *"No, she's not," I said, "but she did tell me that she was expecting you. Won't you have a seat?"*

"Well, how have you been?"

I did not know how much he really wanted to know. I wondered how far back he wanted me to go. Did he want to know about my report cards, or about my tonsils being taken out in the eighth grade? What should I say?

"Fine, for the most part," I answered finally. We continued to sit there and not too much was said. Once in a while we would catch each other sneaking looks at each other.

Finally he said, "Well, now that I'm here, what do you think of me?"

I answered quite uncertainly by saying it was too soon to know. We continued talking and I found out that he would be in town for a week and his main purpose was to visit me. During that week he said that we would do quite a bit of talking.

My mother was surprised to see the two of us conversing as if we were old friends.

"Marsha, you really have taken care of our daughter. It makes me sorry for a lot of things every time I see her smile." Those were not the words of a belligerent father, a father who didn't care until now. Yes, I am seeing him for the first time since my childhood.

While growing up, I never learned anything direct about my real father. In fact I had no idea that I was living a lie. A lie that took about thirteen years to become a reality. How was I supposed to act? Should I act as though we'd known each other for quite a while? I was suddenly brought back to reality when someone said, "Well, Melissa?"

"Pardon me," I said embarrassedly. "What did you say?"

"Your father asked you how your life had been without him," my mother said.

I could not lie and say it has been empty, and it would crush him if I said it was wonderful. "Not half as exciting as it is now," I replied, "not half as much."

During the light conversation between him and my mother I noticed an uneasiness between them. "What did this mean?" I asked myself over and over again. During the week he was with me, I learned quite a bit about him, and in turn he learned about me. That particular meeting was about a month before Christmas. For my birthday in January I got a strange letter and a gift from him. The letter read:

The week I was there was the last week I was in the U.S. I am an Air Force jet pilot and was scheduled to go to Da Nang the next day.

Wow! and I used to think he didn't care. He did . . . he did. There were still questions in my mind, so I wrote him back, but no answer came. It had been that way until June '71 when I grad-

*uated from high school. I got a $100 check and a card. Scribbled on it was:*

*Dear Melissa*
    *No matter what, I'll still love you. I can't explain, but always remember me, always.*

                                                                    *Daddy*

*The card was from an Army hospital in North Carolina. Now it's been eight months since I heard from him. Except for that letter from that hospital, we could not communicate. I found out by other means that he had been shot down over Da Nang and had been seriously injured. He cannot receive any letters that would make him emotional.*

*    Now I do sit around and wonder what has become of him. He entered my life just a year ago, and already he has become a great part. I pray to God that he doesn't leave my life the same way he came in . . . as a stranger.*

"Who wrote that?" said one of the young black men. He was not willing to talk about the paper until he knew. I said it didn't matter but the writer could identify herself if she wished. It did matter to all the black students in the room. And Melissa (I am using a pseudonym) said, "Me." I knew that the curiosity meant respect for the work, but I could drag little out of the class about why it was a good paper. Had the subtleties got through to them or did they like it simply because it told some facts that rang true to their experience? The paper overwhelmed me. Few persons I know—including myself—while suffering such pain can remain so aware of how their words may hurt another.

Once that paper came in, I knew we were on our way.

We weren't. The writing went back to mediocre, except for papers by the two young white men who had started well. Even Melissa was doing pedestrian work. I walked into the room, read a couple of truncated papers like "While laying here" and said they were not enough. Disgraceful work for persons of their age in college. Then I read a paper written by a white girl in another class of mine. She told of early childhood—greeting her father when he came home from work. She teased him into going on a bike ride. When his bike fell over, he injured himself and had been bedridden ever after. She wrote without sentimentality and put the reader in her childish dreams and the tragic action. As I read I noticed several of the black girls looking away melodramatically, acting out boredom. I got mad and said, "Some of you almost went to sleep during that story. I can't believe it meant nothing to you."

One of the black girls said, "I can't identify with that girl. My daddy came home from the factory at night but I couldn't run up and kiss him. He was too dirty."

While she spoke I thought, "What should I say when she finishes?" I decided to let my anger flow.

"I don't believe you. I think you're sulking because I bawled you out about not writing enough. I don't believe you can't identify with a girl who has helped make her father a cripple—whether or not he is dirty or clean or black or white."

There was no support for her from the rest of the class. Just silence. I went on, fearing that I may have lost the black students for the rest of the semester.

Upon reflection, I realize that I had acted with a paranoia common to teachers. I had spoken as if all the students had collapsed when only two girls had written half efforts. In my ranting I was like the corporal I once served under who chastised those of us who showed up for a formation. He cursed us for the absence of the others in our platoon. At home after class that night I discovered that a larger number of long papers had been turned in at the end of that day's meeting than usual. No wonder some of my students had sulked.

☐

Soon after that Byrne Larsen handed me a paper he said he wanted to have read to the class.

*I do not want to write this paper. Only after much debate do I grab my pen with the idea of expressing myself on this paper. I feel forced to somehow tell how I feel. I waited until papers would be criticized in this class because I write with the express intention of having discussion on my subject. Not that the subject hasn't been discussed, but I need some answers in my own mind.*

*I am of what is called the "white" race. I am proud to be who I am, but that would stand, I hope, for whatever race I could have turned out to be. I am not responsible for being born, or for having lived in the town I lived in for a majority of my life. But I am not proud to say I used to live in Dearborn, Michigan. I am not so proud to say the majority of the people in that town believed any race but the "white" race was unwanted. I don't understand a racist mind. My grandfather, who is a Sioux Indian, told me of his troubles in life for being who he was. That shocked me, people hating each other for no reason.*

*Some people might think I'm just another white bastard talking about love because he has never experienced the hardships of being discriminated against. They are right. I have lived in a sterile white culture all my life. But I am inclined to think that there is still hope somewhere for an end to all this stupid hatred. Am I wrong for thinking this?*

*I've only my own experience to tell me what to think. I've had friends of all races and shades whom I think I can live with without the trouble of making a distinction of who is white and who isn't. Maybe I am an eternal optimist who doesn't know better. But I just don't think so. As I walk down the street I usually say hello to most people I come across. Sometimes I feel that people inspect me to see if I qualify for their energy to return my greeting. Most black people will say hello back to me. But it seems like a nervous hello, as if they would really not like to have to bother with me. That gets me uptight. But then why should I expect anything else? I don't really know what to think. That is why I waited so long to write this but it is also the main reason why I did write.*

*I ask—am I wrong to think that a person can be different but because of that difference I don't have to be scared or prejudiced against him?*

*All comments are welcome.*

At home reading that paper I anticipated the hot discussion that would arise. But no, I wanted writing, so I dittoed the paper and handed it out at the end of the next class. I asked for written responses. Glenda Watson wrote this reply:

*Whites are always complaining about the presence of Blacks, and I guess if I was white, I would worry too. Blacks are now at the stage when unity is met and chaos has been suspended. Many Whites are now beginning to realize this and see the young black man's presence very troublesome. This is very actively portrayed in Western's campus life.*

*Living in a dorm it is very evident to see racial tension within dorm directors and assistants but also and especially between residents. Young white girls seem not to be able to comprehend that black unity is necessary for survival. They fail to realize that seeing us in groups tells as much about friendship as defense.*

*Another question which goes through the minds of Whites is—Why can't we stand a "Tom" nigger? Why are Blacks who are in constant surroundings with Whites downed? Blacks who present a quantity of white friends instead of a quality of friends are escaping reality. Most Whites can no longer be looked on as friends but as a threat for the very survival of the black race. How can you be friendly with a race who has enslaved you both mentally and physically? How can you trust a race who has deprived you of your own history and stolen you from your African civilization and culture? At this point it is very difficult to trust someone who seems to be troubled at your very presence. Whites are no longer to be viewed with eyes of belief but instead with serious suspicions.*

That weekend I was scheduled to fly to Asilomar, California, to a teachers' conference. There I told the audience of my experience in this class. I remember a surging feeling as I said I looked forward to getting back to Michigan to read the papers that would answer Byrne's and Glenda's statements. Several teachers spoke enthusiastically of my talk and one said, "I wish I were returning to a class like that."

Next Monday, no responses to Byrne or Glenda. Once again the class had slumped. I knew that at this point I must not turn sour or I would communicate that I expected my students to do badly, and they would meet my expectations. I tried not to show disappointment. I took the best papers to class, read some aloud, had students read others, praised what I could, and waited for improvement. There needed to be a lot, for even the best papers were too short to hold a reader and stay in his memory.

I kept saying "Not enough." Many students said there was enough there for them. I wondered how much of the Blacks' disagreement stemmed from hostility toward a white teacher, how much from that day when I bawled them out, and how much from good judgment—maybe I was wrong. In all those years of studying literature and teaching writing had I developed an inflexible standard for what makes writing powerful? I sagged for a moment. "No," I said to myself. "I've tested my judgment with too many classes."

☐

About eight weeks into the fifteen-week semester Jewell Honeline turned in this paper. I had no doubt that it was powerful.

*Last year I was working at a nursing home. It was divided into a psychiatric ward and a nursing station for old people. The psychiatric ward was the most exciting place I ever worked. I was a desk clerk for the psychiatric ward. Most of the people who came there were junkies and a few young victims. I enjoyed them, maybe because the most of them were young and part of the alienated generation.*

*One day at work I was told to push a button and let the cops in. They came in with a young boy who was only fifteen years old. The child had shot and killed both his parents in a place outside Pontiac. The child was on a court order hold for ten days. He was locked in a room alone. The supervisors had told us he had a mental problem. The next two days he could walk around the ward. He couldn't go behind a pair of double doors, for which I had the keys, that led to the nurses' station. The child and I were talking. He asked for my name and told me his. I wanted bad to ask him about the accident but I didn't. The next few days we were talking and he told me he had never loved his parents.*

*Because they gave him anything he wanted, he never had to earn*
*anything.*
    *We started to walk. I asked him did he want to go on another*
*floor. I felt he could be trusted. As we were walking he told me he*
*knew he would go to jail when he got older. He said he didn't*
*really mind.*
    *I looked up and saw my supervisor coming. I tried to get past*
*her without her seeing me because I was doing wrong. The super-*
*visor called me: "Miss Honeline."*
    *I said, "What?" so loud till she got even madder.*
    *"You know you've done wrong."*
    *The boy said, "She's done nothing wrong here."*
    *She said, "Take him back!" in a raging voice.*
*He screamed as loud as he could, telling her to shut up and leave*
*him alone. She reached for his hand and he took both of his fists*
*and hit her hard enough to knock her down. I told him to come*
*on. He ran to his room. The supervisor got up and phoned the*
*cops. In a few minutes the cops and newspaper men were there.*
*They were taking pictures of the boy. The boy was looking inno-*
*cent as ever. The cops took him away. After everyone left, my*
*supervisor told me to quit my job then or I would be fired. I told*
*her I quit and said, "The boy should have killed you."*

    The class apparently liked the paper, but said little. We made
some suggestions for additions, which Jewell incorporated for the version I have given here. But this paper was the only strong writing I
received at the midpoint in the semester.
    Because the writing was seldom compelling and the students were
freshmen not accustomed to focusing their minds critically, small conversations began to spring up, ruining the discussion. One young black
man—I'll call him Bill—talked with his neighbors while I was trying
to elicit more subtle criticisms of the writing before the class. He was
the most militant of these middle-class Blacks. I had high hopes for
him. Now he was undermining the effort. I said, "O.K., please don't
talk in small groups. If you've got something to say about the paper,
let the whole class hear it. This is a seminar. It depends upon everyone
zeroing in on a paper." In few classes do I have to say this. We moved
on, but soon Bill and his neighbor were muttering again. If I spoke
again would I lose him forever? Would others in the class turn against
me? How much of his intransigence was due to actual interest in what
he was saying, to his youth and inexperience in such intellectual activity, and how much to his hatred of being bossed around by The Man?
He kept talking. The class was slipping away, becoming a shambles. I
looked him right in the eye. "I said I want you to stop talking when
another person is discussing a paper, and I mean that." We held eye
contact for a moment, and there was no giving on either side. The discussion picked up. No more interruptions.

Soon Bill began to miss classes. The group met for two hours twice a week, so his absence cut him out of the central experience of a writing seminar—putting his own work up for criticism and learning from criticizing others, making himself vulnerable. He began missing two out of three classes. I spoke to him. He said fraternity initiation was ruining him. I said this was not an excuse for missing university classes but I could tell he did not understand. He was caught up in the ridiculous, demeaning hazing common in white fraternities thirty years ago. A bright young Black, with some surely founded militant feelings, was wrecking his chances by emulating an outdated white ritual. I considered writing his fraternity or the black administrator who directed the group of "marginal" students Bill belonged to. But I decided against that, once again because I did not want to appear to be singling out Blacks for condemnation.

☐

Altheria Worsham had written a competent case history of her day working in the Health Bureau, but it was wordy. I took it to class, determined to give a lesson. I started in by saying in an unusually careful way that any cuts I suggested were only suggestions, that the writer had the prerogative of retaining what she had written, and that this sort of surgery was always performed by professional writers on their work.

I pointed out that where Altheria had written, "She replied by saying" she could drop the words "by saying." I went on like that for two paragraphs and suddenly the class was taking it away from me. Altheria was busily penciling in the corrections and cuts on her copy. "Wait a minute," she kept saying, "I haven't got that down yet."

The room was full of editors. Often they were finding weaknesses I had missed. They pounced on Altheria's paper, turning it, rending it, flipping it in the air with joy. She didn't mind. She knew she was getting help. We took up subtleties as well as obvious matters. The arguments were pointed and valuable. "This is a funny expression, you better cut it out or change it," said one critic. She was reading Altheria's lines about a man who had come to get the birth certificate of his baby. He said, "I might survive this day but I won't if they don't give me these stamps. I've had to go some of everywhere this morning." Another critic said, "Keep it that way. That's the way he talks." And the same advice was given when the man's language got rougher. It must remain, said the critics, for that is what a guy in his position would say. I agreed. The speech was perfect: " 'What the hell you mean only the mother can get these kids' birth records? I'm their damn daddy. Give me them damn certificates,' he arguably replied." We dropped the *arguably* but kept the rest and the man's later line,

" 'Just fuck it, if I can't get the kids' records ain't no sense me arguing with you, so just fuck the whole damn thing.' "

I left that class buoyant. I had never presided over a better editing session. These kids would come through now.

☐

At the next class several of the black girls stopped the class discussion of a paper with shrieks, laughs, and fast loud remarks I couldn't follow. I doubt that the five white students followed them either. This had happened before. From the first I decided I would allow a lot of spontaneous behavior. I knew the students were undergoing a tough discipline—sitting down to analyze writing out of one's own mind and experience, not simply parroting the critical opinions of a textbook writer. So I let them giggle and guffaw for several minutes. They usually came to an end by themselves. Sometimes I had to step in and ask the class to return to the main discussion.

These were dread moments. The Whites said nothing, sat there thinking I knew not what. Looking back, I think that perhaps these shrieking, shouting sessions were most frequent at a time when six of the girls were writing papers on the level of grade-school kids trying to please teacher with empty proprieties. I think they knew how bad their work looked against the work of the two best white writers and Melissa Cooper. They probably wanted to write strongly, and they were laughing to cover up their embarrassment.

☐

Mary Benet wrote clear sentences in Standard English; her spelling was outstanding. But she hadn't said anything that moved the rest of us. Mary Lou was frightened by the very act of writing down words. She probably felt that finishing a sentence, no matter what it said, was a triumph. Sarah was so quiet and restrained in class and in her papers that I thought she might be stunted. I was giving up on her—a teacher believing his student incapable of anything human. Diane, whom I had liked at the outset because she was not afraid to talk with me in front of the class, was writing bland stuff. In one of her first papers she described her joy in being elected a queen, a guileless tale of winning the popularity contest. No conflict, no tension, no putting us there in the event. Just look at me, they elected me when I sold more chances than anyone else, and I felt so wonderful! Soon she started hanging around after class, and I decided she had determined to be a friendly, if not competent, student.

Ellen was half asleep most of the time. She had joined the group late, missed my talk about honesty, and was full of Engfish. She thought she was superior to most of the other Blacks in the room because she knew bigger words than they did. Earlier when she wrote a paper on how light-skinned girls like her were discriminated against by Blacks in the university, the rest of the Blacks in the class let her know that any such discrimination was based on individuals, not upon skin color. I think they overstated their case and that at the beginning of the course they didn't want us six Whites thinking there was any kind of discrimination in this country besides that of White against Black. Eventually Ellen decided she didn't want to segregate herself, and so she dropped criticism of Blacks and began talking about her blackness.

Ellen began to miss class frequently. One day she looked sickly white—I thought "like the six of us Whites"—and I agreed that she should leave the room. In a stretch of ten class meetings she missed four. I thought she had dropped out. Once before that she had scored with the class with a long description of accompanying teen-aged kids when they stole cars. The tale interested us, I think, because it cited some clever tactics, but generally it read like a slick thriller. There were no authentic, unique details that made the story memorable. By that time Ellen had not done enough good writing that I felt I could point out publicly the weaknesses in her robbery story. So she gained a false confidence. One day I planned the whole class around examples of writing that I thought would help her and several others who were beginning to write grandiloquently. She didn't appear that day. Toward the end of the semester she began attending class regularly, but often appeared drugged. She didn't follow the seminar discussion and would suddenly come on with an angry question or refutation, mis-understanding the matter. Once when she was attacking something I was saying about another student's paper, I said she probably didn't understand because she hadn't been in class when we discussed the subject. She replied that she hadn't missed classes. I said that she had missed many.

One afternoon I asked Diane, the high-school queen, and Sarah to stay after class. I told them they were both writing poorly, that they would have to start putting some of the particular stuff of life into their writing or they were going to impress no one. "Just list the words and actions that led you to a feeling or a conclusion," I said. "Don't worry about telling a connected story, get down some hard facts that speak." Soon after that their writing began to improve.

☐

I was losing sleep. I feared to walk through that classroom door. I saw the room full of hostile Blacks. Their presence had begun to cow me, just as Glenda Watson had said in her answer to Byrne Larsen's paper; I felt vulnerable, but out of weakness. Let them talk, I said to myself, let them giggle and laugh high and croon out their vowels when they say "Man" or "shit" to each other and close us out. Why not? I had read their comments on how it felt to leave their dormitory room every morning.

> *It was really a shock to me to find out that we were in such a minority in the university. I didn't think it was a three-percent deal. I suppose to the Whites this campus is pretty cool but for Blacks I believe you really get a lonely feeling. It's like a fly in milk, whatever way he turns it's a sea of white ... that's kinda scary too when most of us come from all-black high schools or either a fifty-fifty deal. It's a creepy feeling when you walk into a classroom and find there are only two Blacks in the whole class or worse yet only one—yourself. It's not only creepy but bold. How the hell are you going to skip when you're the only damn black face in the class?*

Their chance now. Let them talk and gossip and get off the subject so they'll feel good and pick up a confidence that will help them write.

All my life I have heard Blacks draw out their vowels, but until this moment I had never realized that they do it only when they are happy and relaxed with persons they like. The sound can be brought forth at will, and it is, but it is not ordinarily false. I have always loved the singing quality of that talk. Now I am all the more beguiled because I know it means acceptance and warmth. Not in the next ten years do I expect to hear it from any Black who is talking to me.

☐

Encourage, encourage. One of my fundamentals in teaching. But never meretriciously. Did I have enough good writing from that class to publish it locally and motivate my students to care more about their writing? I knew I didn't, so I went to a young friend who had shown me some of the early writing in his freshman class that was half White and half Black. After Thanksgiving we put out a sixteen-page miniature magazine of our students' best writing. When it was printed, the reactions from my family and friends weren't as positive as they had been for a magazine I regularly publish with a high-school teacher. My friend and I reported to each other that the new magazine also did not score when we read it to our classes. Today I cannot judge it. My friend and I had wanted so much to encourage our students, and we knew that the writings we published represented progress for the writers. But I chalked up another failure in that course, another bad feeling to carry into class with me.

In retrospect it all seems clear: here a mistake, there a right move. But at the time things were opaque. For example, I remember considering this free writing for publication in that magazine:

*Rainy weather used to make me feel so bad. I used to ask my parents why did it rain so much. I would cry when it rained and wish for it to go away. My mother told me never to wish a thing like that. But as I grew up and older the rain made me feel nice. I wanted to sleep all day and night. But to me it's bad, for a lot of my friends want to be with their boy-friends. Next thing you know they're pregnant.*

*Then they don't know what to do—afraid to tell their parents. Too young to get out on their own.*

*The young man doesn't want to get married. So the first thing jumps to her mind is to have an abortion. Then she don't have money neither does he. Now a child may be born in the world with no one to really care about it. A father without a job to take care of anything. A mother too young to get on A.D.C. So I feel the abortion law should be passed. But a child is born. I wonder will this child grow up to love or hate rainy days.*

I felt that paper was a lovely sad prose poem, starting with the rainy weather and coming back to it obliquely. But not fully developed. Many persons might read right past its mystically stated regret, stay with the story on the first level of reality, and find that inadequate. As a piece of writing it doesn't fit any genre. It's short enough to be a poem but written in prose. I didn't publish it.

☐

We weren't moving forward as a group. Some of the Whites were writing worse than before and I sensed that Byrne Larsen—the most thoughtful and sophisticated member of the class—was not learning discipline. His last paper had been sentimental grand stuff about a poor old beggar who might save the world. Bill, Glenda Watson, and a few others had been absent frequently. Two young men had to miss class for draft examinations. Their absences further drained the group of its confidence. Poor writing was coming in and not much of that. An occasional good paper read before the class did not offset the feeling that came over me and, I think, the others. I asked around for papers and received only four in the class of eighteen. Maybe I should have given them all hell. But it's hard to do that when many students are missing sporadically. The day a teacher decides to let loose may be the day that the persons he wants to reach are absent. So I forced: I required the students to write twenty-five minutes during each two-hour period. About half a dozen papers from each session were worth discussing. Now I was moving ahead a little instead of backward.

Glenda Watson went home to care for an injured father. She stayed away for weeks. When she returned I found she had been back on campus over a week but hadn't attended my class because she considered others more important—or harder—to catch up in. I was angry, partly because I had seen that behind her stolid facade she was always thinking. Often her eyes were twinkling. Through her papers she had early established herself among her brothers and sisters as a force they could rally round. At nineteen—I am guessing her age—she was already the black matriarch I had read about. I am sure that the only two black men in the room would not have liked to admit her power, but I am just as sure they would have acceded to it if a crisis had arisen. Glenda's poise was all the more impressive because her silences and her reluctance to engage in small talk with a teacher came from strength rather than fear. I castigated her for missing class and not turning in papers, reminded her that she was one of the best writers in class. She looked at me with neither anger nor fear and returned at the next class meeting with the longest and most complex paper of the course. She said she had picked up the assignment from another student. Her story told of a black youth who resisted his mother's pleas for him to go to college and then was convinced by a militant on the streets that he should go.

A girl who had not scored in class, Mary Benet, turned in a charming story about fearing to meet her boyfriend's aged mother, who confessed to Mary that she had herself been so nervous that she put her watch in the refrigerator.

The writing of Sarah, the quiet one, suddenly flowered. As I had anticipated, when the class began to write at its best, not all the Blacks were writing of blackness. Here is one of her later papers, in its first draft, with no editorial help from the class or me:

> When I was a little girl, I used to go to Bible School every day. The church was about four or five buildings down from our place. This particular afternoon in Bible School our group had just completed singing a verse in a song called "Jesus Loves All the Little Children in the World." While the older group of girls and boys were singing, my attention was pulled somewhere else in the church, over to my Bible School teacher who was sitting beside the piano. She had her hand out as if she were trying to call somebody to help her. The music was so loud from the organ and tambourine that no one would have heard if she had said something anyway. I kept staring at her; she started coughing and gasping for air. I think I was in a state of shock. But in my mind I was saying, "Somebody, please look at Sweetie, something is wrong with her."
>
> She kept putting her hand out and was still gasping for breath as she fell out of the chair on her side. Somebody else saw her. The music stopped. I was still staring. They were making all the children leave the church, but I was still staring down on the floor at Sweetie. They were moving the row of benches back so she could get some air. I was so busy looking that my leg got caught in between two benches. I heard a lady say, "Come on, child.

*Come on, child." Then I realized that she was talking to me. She helped me get my leg out of the benches. Then I went outside of the church and ran home and told my mother that Sweetie was sick.*

*The ambulance came. The people stayed inside the church a long time. When they finally came out of the church, they had Sweetie on a stretcher. She was covered with a blanket from her head to ankles, the only thing you could see was her feet. She had red shoes on with a hole in the toe part. I looked around and everyone was crying; then I realized that she was dead. I sat around all day staring into space and trying to remember Sweetie like she was before she had died, and no one could help her, especially me. At that early age it was my first experience with death. Maybe that's why I don't take it as hard as some people. It sometimes takes other people longer to get over their griefs.*

Melissa Cooper turned in the sequel to her story about her returning Air Force father. He recovered from his wounds, left the hospital, and married another woman. Melissa thought that now she would occasionally see him again as a new-found friend. But the first letter from him said that he could never see her again. His new wife was jealous of Melissa and said if he saw her again she would leave him. In her customary strong way Melissa wrote of trying to accept this new fact of life.

☐

Throughout the course Blacks and Whites freely lauded each other's work. I know I spent more time discussing problems peculiar to the black students' papers but I felt no guilt about the inequity. I expected to do this. I'm sure at times the Whites felt they were being slighted. Except for Byrne Larsen, they talked relatively little in class. I didn't know what was going through their minds, but I didn't worry. For them and for me the experience of being in a minority was refreshing as well as painful. I consider most charges of reverse discrimination silly. In this country where we Whites have kept slaves for centuries and still have not completely liberated men, women, and children from that state, I think Blacks have many special favors coming to them before serious injustice arises.

☐

But the dialect matter worried me. It worries every white teacher of Blacks, and many black teachers as well. Like most English professors with a doctorate I had had considerable training in language and knew that every person in the world and every group of persons speaks differently from every other. Because Blacks as a whole in the U.S. have had less schooling and less rigorous schooling than Whites, their language has not been pressed so hard in the direction of Standard American-English. "Thank God!" I have always said to myself, for I know the pernicious flattening effect of schools—and that includes the university—upon language. Should a Black give up his live, singing dialect because he wants to join the economic world of the White? I think not, but a language question is never that simple. Everyone speaks different languages in different situations. (For example, to succeed in the general world of the press or broadcasting, a person must take on more of a Standard Dialect than is perhaps good for him or his audiences.)

What should I do in the classroom about writers who frequently drop verb endings and use singular verbs with plural subjects? I was convinced that I should do nothing about these matters at the beginning of a course. Take away a person's language when you're trying to get him to write powerfully?

Here's a fact of teaching a black class in a university: the teacher hopes for a long, thoughtful piece of writing and receives this:

> *While sitting here on my bed looking at a pair of black slacks I wonder. Why people today aren't themselfs. These days you see alot of things that you know isn't right. It's ashane to be afraid of your people also others. I want you to take my place for a moment, sleeping in your bed and at 4:00 A.M. awaken by your rommate turning on lights and looking through* [word left out here] *at you.*
>
> *Why do some men and women refained from accepting themselfs as they are??!!*

I received that paper from a university student a third of the way through a course. I have also had an occasional black student who was the most polished and sophisticated writer in a class. But more papers like the above one from Blacks than from Whites.

My reaction was to bawl the writer of that paper out for not doing enough. My patience had ebbed. I was slightly afraid of all those black faces. Now in the calm of my study, looking back on what I consider was finally a successful class, I can see what I should have done. First I should have responded to what the writer was saying. When I saw that sentence beginning "I want you to take my place ..." I should have guessed the writer was about to say something valuable and I should have asked her what experiences led her to write the sentence. But I never led her back to them. I realized that she was afraid of using words and afraid of this class where even her sisters and brothers were writing things so much stronger than she thought she could write. She was the girl who had said she couldn't identify with a white child kissing her father coming home from work. In the last two weeks she began to write papers not great or memorable but good enough to hold the interest of some of the honest critics in that class.

Next I would have to consider the language in the finished paper. I have studied the verb endings in the papers of those black students. The omissions are infrequent and inconsistent. A sentence may read, "She go then and rush through the alley, where she found Jim, and then they both followed Bill the rest of the way." I didn't know what to do with this problem. My instinct was to say let the sentence stand: any American could understand it. I know the breadth and depth of ignorance about language that characterizes the minds of American citizens trained by purist martinets in the schools. "If language is allowed to break down in this way, soon no one will be able to understand anyone else." But I know that language is an agreement between persons: a bit of the code will be taken to mean this and not that. Black people are not having trouble communicating with each other in their dialect. The meaning of *ain't* has always been unambiguous, and "we is going too" is perfectly clear. When an *ed* is left off a verb, almost invariably other cues in the context indicate that the writer is speaking of the past. If there were not such cues, then communication would break down, and someone would devise another dialect that worked.

When it is being used for communication, language is an ingenious instrument. But it has other uses also, one of which is to put down and keep down another group whose language is different in some way from the language of the group in power. Without realizing their intent, those who are horrified at the "illiterate" marks in some Black dialects and express their outrage—whether they be middle-class or upper-class Whites or Blacks—are not trying to improve Blacks' use of language but are pointing out to them and others that it is inferior. Ironically the same oppressors frequently take into their own language the new street expressions of Blacks—*cool, dude, Right on!* "If you associate with them, Tommy, you will not only be getting into dirty neighborhoods full of mugging and dope peddling, but you will eventually ruin your language."

I am proud to say that leaders in the National Council of Teachers of English have taken a strong stand on this issue. In March 1972, the Executive Committee of the Conference on College Composition and Communication passed this resolution:

We affirm the student's right to his own language—the dialect of his nurture in which he finds his identity and style. Any claim that only one dialect is acceptable should be viewed as an attempt of one social group to exert its dominance over another, not as either true or sound advice to speakers or writers, not as moral advice to humans. A nation which is proud of its diverse heritage and of its cultural and racial variety ought to preserve its heritage of dialects. We affirm strongly the need for teachers to have such training as will enable them to support this goal of diversity and this right of the student to his own language.

Many teachers will see this resolution as saying "We should make allowances for Blacks," when it actually asserts the rights of any student, of any color or class, to use his own dialect in school. It sounds like an innocent, democratic statement. Most American teachers would have to turn upside down and inside out to put it into practice.

☐

When I look back on that freshman class I am happy. Finally every student wrote several creditable papers. Probably there was more improvement there than in five other of my writing classes combined. And yet the total production of powerful writing was not what I had hoped for. Most of the Blacks wrote somewhere between their own language and the language of the white schools. When one cannot command his voice, he seldom can command his materials and thoughts.

I think of what the course may have meant to the students—White and Black—in that class who entered it with a paralyzing fear of writing, and I thank the university for going against the elitist tradition in this country and admitting students who were not "qualified for college." Even if some of those students fail other courses and drop out of the university, I believe that probably some day in a business or an organization working for the rights of Blacks, they will not be afraid to put pencil to paper.

I can hear traditionalists crying, "Standards, standards!" and I know what they mean. In that class I feel several students were not challenged by their peers to stretch themselves. But more learning took place in that room than in most classrooms.

With about two meetings left in the semester, one of the young white men turned in a paper from which I give excerpts:

*I suppose I'm resentful towards some of the Blacks in the class because I have been put in the same category as millions of other Whites of the past and present. ... Even if all the other Whites in the world spit in a black man's face, it doesn't necessarily follow that I will. If any man believes it does, he is denying me the right to be an individual human being. He'd be pre-judging me just as many Blacks have been pre-judged, which makes him no better than a racist. ...*

*Ten years ago many, many Whites hated Blacks simply because they were black. That doesn't hold true for me or for many other Whites my age, but we are attributed with these qualities simply because of the color of our skin—no different than the black situation of the past.*

*How many of the Blacks on campus would speak to me on the street not knowing me? Yet how many would speak to another Black? Obviously more would speak to the other Blacks. Why? They know neither one of us, so it must again only be because*

I'm white and the other black. That makes no sense. Since I'm white, I'm bad. I'm to be viewed with suspicion, while the black man is OK because he is black.

In high school I did some volunteer work which enabled me to get to know many Blacks personally. Some of these relationships were rewarding experiences for both the black people and myself. Twice a week two friends of mine and I would visit a family in Detroit near the Chrysler and Mack plants. We got to know this family extremely well and a true friendship was constructed. The only problem was that they were black, we were white. But the problem wasn't caused by them or us. One night we were visiting them for dinner and left at about 9:00 o'clock in the evening. Walking to our car, we were jumped by four black men telling us we didn't belong in that part of town. They left us alone when a car drove by, so we let sleeping dogs lie. The worst news of all came when we visited the family again. Those men had beaten the entire family—the mother and four kids, the oldest nine, and the youngest one-and-a-half-year-old twins. Every one had been beaten. We never got back in that house. All the woman would say was, "White boys aren't welcome." The man hadn't stolen or destroyed a thing. That family was beaten simply for associating with me, a white man.

That was the most asinine, racist, animal-like action I've ever encountered, yet I am the feared one because I am white; and Whites have been cruel to Blacks. I've just shown one instance in which Blacks were racist and wrong, but they are individuals. Each of you didn't beat those kids, so I don't blame you for what happened nor do I fear you. But I am an individual also and can't be blamed for actions of Whites in general or Whites in the past. If Blacks wish not to be pre-judged, I respect that; but I demand the same respect in return.

Once again I handed out the paper at the end of the period and invited written responses. This time there were more, all arrived on the same day. We read them aloud and discussed them. I give a few passages:

Black people are racist—true. We are all racist, but by your paper you portrayed the most projected form of racism there is. You said, "I'm resentful towards some of the Blacks" (all of the Blacks, most likely) "in the class because I have been put in the same category as millions of other Whites of past and present." Who categorized this? Certainly not the poor Black who doesn't have a job or the brains to get an education. How senile! "Whites are to be feared by a Black man." Listen man, you got one hell of a hang-up. You got fear confused with hate. . . .

Here's an excerpt from the paper of one of the quietest, most diffident students I have ever had:

> I come from a small farm in an all-white rural community in lower Michigan. The only experience with Blacks prior to coming to Western has been in sports. . . .
> As I watched and moved into position I saw that our team's defensive end was faked out by the ball carrier. As the runner came at me I was positive I had him, but just that quick he changed direction and I found myself trying to catch up as he raced for a touchdown. He was a Black and he was a great player but what made me angry at the time was that he had faked me out. The whole game continued in much the same manner. After the game ended I was able to congratulate him on his great running. He seemed to me like a pretty good guy but I had only seen him while he was in sports.
> It's true that the Blacks have a bad time getting a good job but I have only heard this and I have very little to do with this except that I am white, and is this reason enough to damn me?

Suddenly the helpless feelings of the Whites had crystallized. Here's an excerpt from another paper:

> I come from a stone white community and I can't help that. What am I to do? Run away?
> My parents aren't too fond of Blacks. I've tried to change that but I can't. My grandfather came from Italy when he was fourteen years old and has lived in Detroit for fifty years. One night a black man was pounding at his door asking to be let in. Minutes later the police shot this fleeing man in the neighbor's yard. For three years my grandfather has slept with a butcher knife under his pillow. Finally he moved out of the city. My father has a sticker on his car that reads, "I fight poverty—I work!" My mother calls the black people "niggers." What can I do?
> Perhaps our generation will turn the tide. But as it is right now, we'll never get people to love others they've been taught to hate. . . .

The meeting at which those papers were read became a shouting match. But these young people had come to know each other. After they had seen the pain and love and understanding each writer had shown talking of his family or of hunting or baseball, they couldn't hate each other blindly. There was anger and confrontation. Persons listened long enough to hear and face what I think seemed to all of us at times the unfaceable. I can't forget the moment when the black students forgot us, the white minority. Lenora Baird, who had been one of the most charitable Blacks toward Whites, said, "I don't think Blacks and Whites will ever come together."

"Sure, you're right," said Bill. "But what we gonna do?"

"We could go back to Africa," said another student.

"You crazy?" said another young man. "You know those Africans never gonna accept us either."

"Well, we got to go somewhere."

"Yeah, but where could we go?"

At the next meeting we read two good short papers and another comment on black-white relationships. I said, "Do you want to discuss this again?"

"No," said Bill smiling ruefully. And others, Black and White, joined him in refusing.

When Glenda Watson and Pearl Sullivan stopped in my office the next day to pick up their grades and their writing folders, they told me that they had recommended my class to friends as one in which a student would learn something about writing. Other friends reported taking writing classes in which they spent most of their time reading literature and sociology.

When they said goodbye they were friendly, even Glenda, the contained matriarch. I touched Pearl on the shoulder. I wanted to embrace the girls as I often want to embrace black persons. I admit this feeling without shame, knowing it is partly motivated by the feeling that I am one of those in the powerful position in society and they are not. I feel instinctively that they need my comfort. Most Blacks would be incensed to know that. It is a fact that I am from the more powerful group and they from the less powerful. I hope some Blacks will feel like touching me out of the need to comfort one of the blind who have never known fully what they have done to others.

*Chapter 9*

# Teaching Teachers

☐

... I am firmly persuaded that every unnatural activity of the brain is as mischievous as any unnatural activity of the body, and that pressing people to learn things they do not want to know is as unwholesome and disastrous as feeding them on sawdust.

Bernard Shaw, quoted in *G.B.S.*:
*A Full Length Portrait*, by
Hesketh Pearson (New York: Harper, 1942), p. 12.

□

I have said earlier that I was afraid when I went to college. Fear is natural when persons come together to perform and be compared. For twenty-five years I have been nervous when I face a class on the first day.

In the summer of 1971, when I walked into a room in the University of Missouri in Columbia, I found my class of high-school and junior-college teachers chattering in such a friendly way that I knew we would get off to a beautiful start, but I was unsettled because they were relaxed and I tense. My one-week workshop in teaching "composition" was the third in a course that had included the teaching of modern grammar and literature. I said, "Go ahead, keep talking. I'll wait a few minutes for late-comers." Five minutes went by. I had to speak loudly to get their attention. They all turned to me then as if I had interrupted —which I had—with looks that I read to be saying, "Oh, he's here now. I wonder what he'll be like."

I had to break in and say the first thing I want to say to any group of persons becoming writers. I'm embarrassed to talk or write about it because it sounds soft. It is the matter of trying to be truthful. I was going to take these teachers through a course in which they were to follow what my freshmen do in a writing course, so that they could know intimately what this method can do for a person and how he feels struggling in it. First I read to them a sample of the sort of writing that is bred in high-school and college classes in which students are writing what they think the teacher wants to read.

## OUR OBLIGATION

*At the present moment in history, the United States is engaged in a war with the armies of North Vietnam, a country—or rather a part of a country—in Southeast Asia which has . . .*

I said, "Now that's news to Americans today (summer of 1971), isn't it? And how helpful to make that academic distinction—North Vietnam is not all of Vietnam. I'll read a paragraph farther on:"

*. . . a soldier in this war may experience fear and impending doom while his friend at home is whiling away his or her hours in casual play. And yet when the friend at home reflects upon the experience of the soldier on the bloody battlefield, he or she can only realize that there is a vast difference between the two, and that if the world is ever to become a better place in which to live, such reflection must go beyond mere idle thought and effectuate in deeds which end the scourge of war forever.*

"Omygod yes," I said, "if the world is ever going to be a better place in which to live. That must be what the teacher wants. No truths there that belong to anyone, rather to everyone; and therefore no one wants to hear them again and forever. And that 'he or she' bit, and 'vast difference,' and 'effectuate.' The language does not belong to the writer.

"In the past I have been more responsible as teacher for that kind of phoniness than the students who wrote it. And so with most teachers. For where would a human being learn to write like that? Surely not on the streets or in the kitchen. At school, that's the place. No matter how much any teacher might condemn that writing, it was learned in school.

"Now I'll read you a paper written by a high-school student taught by John Bennett at Central High School in Kalamazoo, Michigan." I read the following:

## GOT A LETTER THIS MORNING

*I opened up the light blue envelope and unfolded the white paper.*

*". . . the whole world has had enough of me. I've lost too many friends in too short a time. I led my patrol into a Viet ambush. Three men dead. I'm sorry, but I don't really think I'll be coming home."*

*I forced myself to read it again, and put the letter back in the thin airmail envelope and laid it under a few sweaters in my drawer. Then I forgot about it. I went to work and came home. My brother Jim made some fudge. It didn't taste good since it was instant fudge out of a frosting mix. We sat down at the kitchen table and began modeling with it.*

*"Hey Tina, this is what my gym teacher looks like." It was a glob of chocolate with features carved into it.*

*"Yeah," I said. "And this is what he looked like after he got in a fight." I hit the fudge with my fist, flattening it. We both began laughing.*

*"Pizza." Jim flattened the fudge out on the table. Then after carefully scraping it up off the table, he tossed it up so it hit the ceiling. The phone rang. Still laughing at the mess my brother had made of the ceiling, I answered.*

*"Hello?"*

*"Hello Tina. This——(mumbled)."*

*"Just a minute." I shut up my brother. "I'm sorry, who?"*

*"Mrs. Benson."*

*"Oh, hi."*

*"Have you heard from my son lately?"*

*"Well, yes, I got a letter from him just this morning."*

*"I did too. He said he's feeling awfully bad. He hasn't got any mail for about three weeks. Have you been writing him?"*

*"Yeah, that's what he said. I can't figure it out. I've sent him quite a bit."*

*I always hate for her to call. She'll tell me he's dead. Yesterday I got another letter, too. "Please write so I know what the world is like so I can get back to shooting little people I don't even know."*

*I think ahead to when he's going to come home and how long it's going to take to get him back to normal.*

*Now for my personal analysis—I'm messy. My bedroom is so messy that I've had to sleep on the couch in the basement for the past three months.*

I said to the class of teachers:

"When I first read that paper, I thought, 'Where's the ending? Something's gone wrong. John Bennett—the high-school teacher I work with—must have sent me only half the paper.' The last lines seemed to me completely off the subject. But on second reading I understood. I was supposed to keep separate the soldier's and the girl's experiences though they were piled one on the other. And then to bring them together to see the writer was comparing the triviality of her daily life with the terror of the soldier's.

"When a person is bearing down as hard as he can to tell truths, great things happen. His sentences pick up rhythms. He slides into a style that fits his subject. One true, telling detail breeds another.

"In this course I'm asking you to try to speak and write truths. I know that you won't always succeed. We try for truth and later what we have said seems false to us. But the attempt changes the character and quality of what we say and think. In this class I'm going to try to speak truths. I know you'll find some hypocrisies in what I say, but I'll be trying. I ask you to try, too."

"But who would want to speak truths all the time?" said one of the teachers. "Truth can be cruel, you know."

"Sure," I said. "White lies are sometimes necessary, but when we should speak them is hard to decide. The habit of lying to please others can be as damaging as the habit of speaking truths can be productive."

One of the teachers complained that it's easy to ask for truth but no one knows what it is. "All writers lie at times," he said. "You're going to hold us to higher standards than many professional writers observe?"

"I won't *hold* you to that standard," I said. "But I will ask you to try to maintain it as steadily as you can. For truthtellers, a lower standard than the highest they are aware of is always damaging."

I went on to other matters: "There will be no tests in this course. And no grades until the final one at the end of the course when I look over all the work you have done. But don't fear that this final grade will sneak up on you. Day after day your work will be in front of the class, commented on by all of us here. Some of it will not receive full examination—praise, analysis, suggestions for reworking; but you will get a good idea of what others think of your writing. And as you criticize the work of others you will be unconsciously criticizing your own. At the end of this week we have together, I will choose what I think is the best writing and ask you to prepare it for publication in a little mimeographed magazine.

"At this point in a course I always say what I have just said to you. If I don't my students will rightly fear they are being trapped. Many teachers before me have begged them to tell truths. When they told one the teacher didn't like, they found their grades going down. But if through the course all the students have been commenting on papers, the teacher cannot easily go against the opinion of the class to indulge a prejudice."

☐

Then I said to the teachers:

"Now I want all of you to write freely for fifteen minutes whatever comes to your mind, as fast as you can, not stopping to think; to plan; to consider grammar, spelling, or mechanics. If you feel blocked and can't write a word, look at whatever is before you—wall, clock, house across the street—and begin to describe it. You will soon find your thoughts moving. Let your minds and pens run wherever they will. Do that twice, fill at least four sheets of large notebook-sized paper, maybe more.

"When you turn in the papers, I will look them over quickly and excerpt the phrases or passages that strike me as good, for whatever reason—style, surprising ideas, feelings, information. Maybe just because they are straightforward, economical statements not in Engfish. Then I will present them dittoed for class discussion.

"These are free writings. I don't expect them to be consistently great. Maybe some of the papers won't contain one sentence or phrase that strikes me. If so, I will excerpt nothing. No sweat. No failure. These are free writings to see what happens. There will be more free writing. Somewhere in the first three meetings I always find at least one remarkable passage by every student."

☐

I asked the teachers to do the free writing in any empty classroom in the building and return in half an hour. They were meeting with me all day for five concentrated days. Ordinarily I have students write at home, or anywhere else they feel comfortable and will be free from interruption.

I gave the students an hour break and began reading what they had written.

*But first of all I'd cut down the cedars in the yard. Of all the trees in the world I still hate cedars the most. Try mowing a yard with a push mower in your bare feet and having to pull cedar stickers out. Cedars grow on poor land. Cedars are sure signs of scraggly homes. Cedars grow on land that has been strip mined, where no other plants with any class will grow. Cedars hurt at Christmas time. Cedar stickers stay in the carpet all the year no matter how often I vacuum. My husband loves cedar trees. He cut a 12-foot cedar tree for Christmas. When he got it in the house, he had to cut two feet off the top. It was either that or move the tree to mid-fireplace where there's an air grate going to the second floor. Wouldn't it have been great to remove the grate and have two feet of Christmas tree in the upstairs bedroom, angel and all?*

I thought, "How could she do it? Get that bite and detail without having considered the subject for weeks?"

I read on in other papers. When I saw the first sentence of the one printed below, I thought, "Here we go with the apologies." By the time I had read the last sentence I was smiling.

*Boy, am I a slow starter at writing. I've had two English papers to write at summer school. They've both taken me a couple of days of thought and a day of writing. Funny that I knew they were good English papers (analytical) before I handed them in. They sounded kind of literary but I wonder if they were written in Engfish. Well, I don't actually wonder because I could pick out some Engfish sentences for you right now. I was telling the truth, though, on the papers. Let's say I was testing my own critical powers and didn't consult anybody else's opinion or an outside source. I said, "Come on, subconscious, come on, inductive powers —get busy." It's a start, anyway. I feel that part of my masquerade in life is to have people think I'm especially smart because I went to X school in the East. Me—a farm girl from upstate New York. Little do they know that at my school I was less than average—nope, I was average, I guess. . . . Why do I say X College? I'm trying to keep from bragging (I almost put quotation marks around that word, that's a form of bragging, too)—I went to Vassar College and am proud of it.*

I read another paper and excerpted these lines:

*Cheri cried again yesterday when I left. She even ran after the car in what I think was a conscious theatrical act. Anyway, it*

*tears me to shreds. I feel like hugging her. She has two and a half
teeth missing. And she's determined to have long hair by the time
she starts to school and right now it usually strings and tangles
around her impish face. She keeps asking me if I really like her
freckles or if they are ugly. She laughs like water over ice cubes
in the summer. She's beautiful.*

*David is my other loneliness right now. He's nine and deep,
more intense and more tense. I made him more nervous. I'm sorry
for that. His laughter is a trifle more strained unless we are alone.
Then he says things like, "I'm so damned tired" and looks at me
and laughs a confident sort of chuckle that makes me know that
we do have a great relationship in spite of our short tempers in
moments when things don't go our way.*

☐

Then I read these lines in another teacher's paper:

*This week is going to be absolutely killing for me for the simple
reason that I cannot write. Of course I felt week before last that
last week would be terrible too because I had never in all my
years of teaching done one thing with the new grammars. ... I
may wish I had Mr. V. hiding in a closet somewhere so he could
come out and explain why this or that just cannot possibly be
"the way it has always been." ... I said I wasn't going back to
school in the summer again when I could be out on my beautiful
farm enjoying my flowers, the cattle, etc.*

"I cannot write." I have heard that sentence again and again from
teachers of English. Several have written me that they think this is a
belief shared by a majority of English teachers in the country. Some of
them were in my class, scared. They did not feel like making themselves vulnerable to me and the other teachers in the room. That is
why a method of teaching like this one is apt to work: it asks the student to commit himself, but freely—without any defined expectations.
And the teacher lets everyone know he will choose only those passages
of writing which strike him as good, and he will not comment on the
others. Under those circumstances I have customarily found only two
or three students in a class not able to make themselves vulnerable
from their strength.

☐

On the next day I asked the teachers to begin to keep notebooks in
which they recorded thoughts and experiences that struck them. Not
stupid diaries in which the writer says he met the most wonderful

person in the world and feels shivers going up and down his spine every time he thinks of her, but hard statements that let the reader see persons in action so he can judge the writer's judgment of them. When I first collected the notebooks of one of the teachers who worked at a nearby college, I found most of her entries stated her ambivalent feelings toward the course. She wanted to like it, but she also wanted to let me know that she looked with suspicion on the then current "encounter" or "sensitivity" kind of training. Her writing was as unsure as her opinions. It lacked force. So I did not reproduce any of it for the class and did not comment on it. Her remarks made me uncomfortable and defensive, but I vowed I would welcome her as an antagonist who would keep the class from becoming subservient.

☐

When the journals came in again, I looked first for the one belonging to my antagonist. One of her early long entries was a vacillating comment about her earlier remarks about people who worship freedom for itself. Then apologies for talking so much about that subject. Next, this entry:

> *Three or four years ago I was reading Willie Morris's* North toward Home. *The first part of the book is about his early years in Yazoo City, Mississippi, a town about fifty miles from the town I grew up in. I was reveling in the anecdotes, the descriptions, the characterizations, and hardly even looked up when my two sons, then twelve and seventeen, walked in. But boys that age intrude, so as a concession to my concentration they asked me what I was doing.*
> *"I'm reading a book," I said, "and it fills me with nostalgia."*
> *"What's nostalgia?" John, twelve, asked.*
> *And Chuck, who at seventeen had lived with his expatriate parents much longer, replied with feeling: "It's the state flower of Mississippi."*

On the succeeding page of her journal she had written:

> *I knew I was lucky to have my daughter confide in me, but listening to talk about sixteen and seventeen-year-old boys is enough to make someone invent a generation gap.*
> *One afternoon I said to her, "Now look, Judi. I've heard all I want to hear today about boyfriends—yours, Susan's, or anybody else's. When you have something else to talk about, come back in, but until then why don't you go on and let me get to work?"*
> *She looked only a little crestfallen—it hadn't been a good day anyway—as she went out of the room. I'd hardly resumed*

*what I was doing when she came back in and settled herself in a chair near me. I looked up at her.*

*"I think the church today is irrelevant," she said.*

*I sighed and said, "Let's go back to boyfriends."*

In the margin of her journal Mrs. Wendell (not her real name) had written: "Must quit writing these trivial anecdotes about the children." I thought they were first-rate, so I dittoed up a number of them and read them to the other teachers. They broke up in laughter. I said that Mrs. Wendell had depreciated these entries but that I thought she should write more. Together they might make a book that would speak to beleaguered parents. I added that she knew how to write humorously, a gift to be cherished. Like so many of us, Mrs. Wendell wanted to write something grandly intellectual—she was a college teacher. But her gift is humor and she commands it most powerfully, as I would expect, where she lives. That is where most useful books are written.

From that moment on, when Mrs. Wendell looked at me, the suspicion was gone from her eyes. Before, there had been a bemused, haughty look every once in a while, and I had felt lowered by it.

☐

One woman in that class wrote about her father.

*My father worked hard all his life. During the depression of the thirties he raised hogs so he could pay off the Land Bank Loan and not lose his farm. He must have walked hundreds of miles carrying a five-gallon bucket of swill to each of the sows who farrowed in the place to her liking. He could have penned them all in one hog-house and cut down considerably on the work, but he had the theory that it was better for the sow to make her nest where she wanted because it would probably be on clean ground and there would likely be less chance for infestation of the new litter. Thus, when he found her he built a shade and unbegrudgingly carried her breakfast and supper.*

When I finished reading that paragraph aloud to the class, the praise began. I think six persons said why they thought it was strong. In different ways several students said that the paper was persuasive because it claimed nothing but rather recorded telling facts. I finished the commenting by saying I thought this was a tribute of the first order, and that it would be proper and fulfilling if all of us could write such statements about persons we loved. At that point the writer started sniffling, said, "I'm sorry, but he just died a year ago," and left the room. When she returned in about ten minutes I would have none of her apologies. I thought we should all cry for such a man.

Earlier in the discussion there had been an argument about that paper. I let it go on, though it violated the rule that only positive comments should be made during the early meetings of a writing course.

"I'm not an expert, but that word *infestation* doesn't sound right there."

"Maybe she means infection?"

"No. That's what I mean. That's what farmers call it."

"The word didn't bother me at all."

"Well, it's not serious, but it's out of character with the other words in the passage. Sounds like what a professional would say."

"But maybe farmers use it—then it's the truth that she's putting down."

"I don't care if it's true to life—to most readers it won't seem so."

That debate lasted about twice as long as I indicate here—I don't remember everything that was said. But after about five minutes I said, "Well, the author now has several opinions before her. She will have to decide what word to use. I think we've done all we can for her. It would be wrong to try to decide for her—perhaps by vote—exactly which word she should use. She has intentions and feelings that we cannot have because we are not speaking of our experience."

□

On the second day of that class Ruby Warren turned in this free writing:

*I always love to be on campus—or so I tell myself; I think I really have mixed emotions about it. Do I fit or do I just want to fit—to roll back the years and present the vigorous, self-confident image I think I see in the college-age youngster?*

*Well, I walk along campus from white building to white building or red building and I think of all the traditions they hold. But I keep watching the young kids, especially the girls. I don't notice what they wear although I am vaguely conscious of whether they have legs showing or are panted to the ankle. What I notice most is their gaits, how they seem to ride along smoothly on their straight, sturdy legs. Their spines are straight and their bellies flat. Their muscular thighs seem to swing forth with an unconscious rhythmic movement, free-wheeling from the hip joint, in turn the lower leg swings from the knee, then the ankle sort of pumps forward and pushes the foot down. But they don't stop to think about how beautifully they walk. If they did, they would probably get self-conscious and awkward. I watch these young girls and sometimes boys walk and I try to walk that way too. I look in every mirror or window glass I pass, trying to see if I am riding along on straight, muscular legs and if my spine is straight and my belly flat, and my rear tucked over. How I would like to walk this way enough to make it an unconscious habitual gait in my life.*

*You can't notice walking forever, and sometimes you see the faces of the walkers as well as the legs. Last night I saw a short Oriental girl, clad in blue jeans and a blue cotton blouse, coming from the Fine Arts Building. I had just read a sign on the door that said play practice was being held. Well, this little girl, whose eyes had been clipped to make her look American, had reddish smudgy circles under her white eyelid makeup. I wondered if she had been crying because the rehearsal had gone badly or if her director had bawled her out. She looked sad and all that but her legs still moved in that smooth poetic way that suggested a sense of well being. I guess her gait was automatic and was not conscious of her hurt feelings.*

About that writing my teacher students said exactly what I had felt as I read it. They were amazed at its professionalism—and written so fast! They found the move from subjectivity to objectivity exciting. They admired the description of the students walking. They liked the pointed ending: the suffering girl who retained her easy stride. One objection: "my rear tucked over" didn't sound right. Ruby changed it to "tucked under."

☐

Once we had all heard Ruby Warren's paper on the campus gait, I knew the class was moving and nothing could stop it. For her success was bound to breed more success in the writing of the others. She was just another school teacher. They knew that. They had lived with her through two weeks of a course in grammar and a course in literature and could see she was a middle-western American like the rest of them, for some a much older woman who should be hardened and narrowed by middle-class society. But here was this paper. So she was special, and because they were much like her in many ways, maybe they were special. Maybe at times worthy of reverence from others. I hadn't been impressed with her when I first heard her speak. She had a studied manner, I thought. I have a slipshod manner, I suppose. I look around for phrases and throw the tries at my listeners. (Joyce says this is probably a strength in my teaching. I don't come down from heights of language to my students.) I came to love Ruby's slow, careful way of talking because I expected always she was about to say something perceptive and new.

In that class and others I have been teaching lately, most of us sit around anticipating that when others speak up or we hear their writing read aloud they will say something exciting and new. They don't always do that. But our set is different from the set so many students and teachers bring into classrooms. We are not expecting to be bored. We notice good things when they appear. We are listening, not looking out the window. And because we know others are anticipating good things from us, we try hard to be truthful.

On the third day, Steve McCauley wrote this entry in his journal:

### MARY CALHOUN

*Mary Calhoun lived a block down the hill from Dutch. Dutch lived two blocks from the river because no white man would dare live closer to the river than two blocks. And Dutch even loved the river.*

*He used to take me down the bank to his boat on a well-traveled path through nigger town. Our path took us past Mary's house where we'd stop to talk.*

*Mary Calhoun sat eternally it seemed on the front porch of the Calhoun shanty. The house was small; Mary was immense. She was the fattest, blackest woman I ever saw in my life. She sat there enthroned on her porch on the peak of the hill that overlooked Water Street. She was always laughing, she said, because life was such a circus, and if it was, Mary should know, because from where she sat she could see it all.*

*Every time she laughed, the porch shook. It was on props of uneven, upended lumber resting on stones that Pete, her husband, had laid for her when he built the house. How could Pete have known what a large, laughing lady Mary would become? Or that shaking the porch would become for Mary as important a part of her amusement as the laughter itself?*

*Some people said that one day the porch would get her; and it's true that every time I saw Mary the porch would be a fraction of an inch farther from the bricks. I began to expect to find her, each time we descended the hill, oozing out from under a heap of wood and bricks. I pictured myself bending down through the fog of settling dust and looking for signs of life—and hearing Mary laugh.*

*The path that continued past the house was not our path, it was Mary's. She lives on a sort of sub summit of the hill so that anyone coming down that way had to veer in a new direction starting there. The path was remarkable, a black three-foot deep V-worn trench, shiny and treacherous. Dutch and I helped wear that trench with our feet. It was a beauty.*

*Mary had not been down that way for ages. She would have rolled. There was no other descent. And she was too fat to climb, so she sat on the porch and watched her folk and her river roll by below.*

*I hardly knew Pete because he was always away. Pete had chickens and he loved to fish so he divided his time between the hen yard and the river. But, as I say, I seldom saw him because the hen yard was distant and the river was big, so we seldom passed.*

*Mary wouldn't let Pete keep chickens behind the house because that's where she did her washing. Somehow Pete had toted an electric wringer washing machine up or down the hill. He kept her in what luxury he could. But he had never gotten electricity up or down the hill. So Mary set the machine behind the house and washed in rain water. Mary always washed after a good rain.*

*One morning it rained and Pete didn't come in off the river. He had died in the boat. After the rain they found him and brought him up, carried him up the steep, deep worn dirt path and gave him back to Mary.*

*We thought, Dutch and me, that Mary would die, so up the hill we kept the windows closed even after the rain stopped, because we were afraid we'd hear her crying. It scared me to think of Mary not laughing. It terrified me to think of her crying. I was afraid I'd hear her scream climbing the hill, so I stayed shut up above with Dutch and sorted tackle.*

*That evening Mary put out a wash. When it was done and on the line the sun set.*

*Next day, Dutch and I went down. Mary was on the porch and Pete was away, as usual. We mumbled awhile, then Mary looked at me and said, "You got nice hands, boy, you ought to play the piano." I asked her what we could do. She laughed. She said, "Just keep coming down. The river'll still be here and so will I."*

*That day after we went down Mary's path and set out in the boat, Dutch and I didn't blow as much as usual, sharing secret wisdoms I guess, but we laughed as much as ever. It was good to know we didn't need to worry about Mary Calhoun.*

*I have a new fantasy. The porch will never get Mary. It'll carry her, just as usual, even when the props give way; she'll just kind of glide down (She'll be laughing, of course) and land wumpf! right in the trough and ride it (laughing) to the river. The porch will be her barge and she'll set about collecting rain water and putting up clean sheets for sails.*

*It's a silly thought, I guess, but I see Mary Calhoun as a rider, not a sinker, who survives through wisdom.*

*I admire her. She is wise—and hasn't even read Whitman. I've read Whitman, but I think I need to live longer.*

*I play the piano now.*

I thought that was bringing a person alive. Later I will say more about this paper.

Again and again I have had that experience in writing classes: the students write better when I have assigned them no special task. Undoubtedly Mary Calhoun came to Steve's mind on that third day of our course. He wanted to write about her. He was ready to write about her. We talk so much about motivation in education, about its fundamental powers, but we make assignments as if motivation could be turned on at will by the student or supplied by a short talk by the teacher. The springs of human action are more manifold and mysterious.

I try now in my teaching to deal with things that work, to proceed not on traditional educational theory. I can hear some professors saying, "Now your pragmatic approach—" I don't want a name like that for it because I don't see any longer a choice between this approach or that in theory. I see only teaching so that students do and say and build things that count for them, for me, and for others. There is the test of the teaching and that is the only test I am interested in in schools. If the course is in writing, what do the students write? If the course is biology, can the students write, photograph, draw, construct, say, or do something that counts for them, their teacher, and others? Can they do something significant with a growing organism? If the student is a history major, his school work should make him talk or write so he increases the understanding and awareness of others by his historical sense. Life today should be made more vivid by his knowledge. If not, then he has had a failing history course taught by a failing history teacher.

Traditionally school is thought of as a place for preparing for life, acquiring skills and knowledge that will be applied at a later date—a foolish aim for a woman or man who has about seventy-five years to live on this earth. It is common for persons who go to graduate school to spend upwards of twenty years in schools. No payoff during those years? No joy? No meaning? Only preparation?

☐

A reader may be thinking that this course I am describing sounds like fun, but when am I going to get down to business? When are my students going to do something more than just write freely what comes to their minds? They need to master some disciplines that will get them through the realities of their jobs.

Even in my sparse description it should be clear that the teachers who were my students have been learning the discipline of writing. But what they have been doing seems so natural and so much a part of a whole, human act that it may not appear as disciplined behavior. For example, Steve Miller turned in this journal entry:

*Everyone seems so close, yet so far away. Room 104 is empty now, or is it? The people are gone, but something remains. Every-*

one and everything in this room has become tied up. Oh, crap, I can't write this, people are returning, the quiet is gone, the room has lost its shape. What to do—where to go?

The air outside is cool or was cool. It awakened me rather abruptly this morning as I half ran to class. I wish I'd walked; it would have made the world seem nicer.

The tar seeped up around my shoes. I could feel them shick-shick as I pulled away. The telephone poles were markers. They moved by me as I stood still. It was effortless but exhausting. On and on, it was great. The sun was everywhere. Every thought was forever. I'd feel light and heavy, tired and strong, wild and lazy, but slow. It's funny how when I run by myself I feel slow and then I decide to go one final telephone pole length. All out—but slow. Then nothing: my head would swim and spin. My thoughts would be gone. Everywhere would be relief. My entire body would pulsate and I'd wobble on my weak/strong legs. But I felt good. Then I'd be able to think again; slowly the world would settle down, slow down. I'd be able to rest.

Think I'll run tonight.

Several critics in the class suggested that the third paragraph held together, said something clear and connected by itself. Steve agreed, and when he turned in the writing for publication in the magazine we published at the end of the course, he had not only cut out the first two paragraphs, but edited the third to tighten it up and make its verb tenses consistent. His revised version:

The tar seeps up around my shoes. I can feel them shick-shick as I pull away. The telephone poles are my markers. They move by me as I stand still. It's effortless, but exhausting. On and on, it is great. The sun is everywhere. Every thought lasts forever. I feel light and heavy, tired and strong, wild and lazy, but slow. It's funny how when I run by myself I feel slow and then one final telephone pole length all out. Then nothing: my head swims and spins. My thoughts gone. Everywhere is relief. My entire body pulsating and wobbling on my weak strong legs. But I feel good. After a time I can think again; slowly the world settles down, slows down, I'm able to rest.

Think I'll run again tonight.

That is the kind of discipline that counts. It shapes and transmutes. It comes from listening to oneself as well as others. It makes over and the making is creation, not punishment.

□

That one-week course for teachers of writing that summer was not a waste of our lives. Some of their comments will slip from my memory but many will remain. The young woman who had not been present for the first day's discussion of trying for truth produced free writings dull in every way. She was enthusiastic about the class but her journals were dead. On the third day I took her into another room and told her I wanted her to go back to free writing, to try for truths as hard as she could, and to write so fast she couldn't stop to plan or be self-conscious. In forty-five minutes she was back with this paper:

> The house across the street has an interesting style—a white porch, five sets of windows. The ones directly above the porch have only two in the set, all the others are a series of three, one larger one in the middle, with a smaller one on either side. The house is red brick, a sure sign of Missouri. My sister-in-law who lives in Chicago told me how difficult it was to buy a house there with even a brick facade. I remember too how the kids from Burlington, Iowa, would come to St. Louis (we sometimes chartered a bus for them) and they would be amazed at the brick homes. They thought the people with brick homes really had the money. Here I had lived my whole life in St. Louis or nearby. I had lived in a brick home. I had not realized that not every city had brick homes or even brick streets.
>
> Today in my hometown, Buena Vista, we still have brick streets. The restorers of this place, one of the first cities in Missouri, have made sure the brick streets stayed there. Each time I go near this old capitol building the car just rumbles over the bumpy bricks. This old building and even the antique shops are all constructed of brick.
>
> My dad used to lay bricks. I enjoyed standing there and watching him or others place a brick in position, then smooth down the mortar, then to another brick. Brick after brick, yet unevenly spaced.
>
> I found out once why bricks are not placed one on top of the other straight-in-line as bathroom tile I think is—at least these strips of tile that are already put together. How could they still have some holding power? Can't you just see all the mortar in one straight column?
>
> Take a look at the top of the radiator. That is how the bricks would look—not even artistically placed. Look at the venetian blinds and see how perfectly parallel the slats are. The tapes carefully hold these slats in place. None turns unless they all turn—all at the mere pulling of the cord. Sometimes I wish people were like that. Then I could predict their responses. I wish I could have the teachers in the English department so pro-

*grammed to teach composition. I can always do it on paper. On Day A—Jane, Cheryl, Sue will teach composition and here's the lesson to be taught. This is really stupid for me to say because if I had my way I wouldn't do it like that. But my principal, who taught English for many more years than I have says it must be done. She's going around next year to make sure the teachers are doing it—her way which she wants to be "my" way. I don't know how I can set up an English program for the sophs, juniors, and seniors—especially the comp program and make her happy. Maybe I'd best forget about keeping her happy. If necessary, why not place the game of introducing the paper like Macrorie gave us and have this put out monthly so the principal can see that the kids are writing in their English classes. How can I teach English teachers this new approach without having mass confusion and total insecurity? They don't know how to teach composition— they get all uneasy about it, and so—literature all the way! How can you hire one teacher to teach all the composition and yet how can I supervise all their classrooms when I too have three classes of my own to teach? My first reaction is to say, "Hell with it all," but I can't do that when nine hundred students are the losers.*

When a student stalls or can't get going as powerfully as the others, I return him to free writing and he breaks loose from his fears because he knows nothing is expected of him but truth. I hesitate to say that the dozen or so students who at the halfway point in a class have failed to get started have all responded well when asked to return to free writing. It sounds incredible. But they have. I record the fact.

□

Knowing that we had only five days in that workshop for teachers and wanting to get a lot of writing out of them, I asked for four free writings and then nothing but entries in journals—any kind they wanted to make: long, short; objective, subjective; criticism, narrative; whatever. Some of their best entries were short and concentrated, like poems. Steve McCauley wrote:

*A bunch of us were sitting around in the apartment talking about brothers and sisters. Ben turned to me and asked if there were any other kids in my family.*
*"No," I let slip, "I'm a lonely child."*

Ruby Warren wrote:

*Buy a journal, he said. Carry it. How can I have been so blind? All these years I've carried paperbacks so as not to lose a thought while I sat under the hairdryer or waited in those antiseptic dungeons inhabited by the old, the infirm, the ill, the injured, the medical supply salesmen. Why did I never think before that I shouldn't lose my own thoughts?*

Jan Sharp wrote:

> *I watched out the window*
> 
> *A local cop*
> *stopped*
> 
> *an old man in a pickup*
> *going*
> 
> *the wrong way*
> 
> *on a one way.*
> 
> *The old man opened the door*
> 
> *and SPAT*
> *a pointed tobacco cud*
> 
> *at the pavement.*
> 
> *When the cop reached the truck*
> 
> *he kept disdainfully*
> 
> *sidestepping*
> 
> *the wad.*

These observations recorded quickly in a student's notebook may seem small and therefore trivial. The excitement they generated suggests otherwise. They project surprise, an element ordinarily foreign to the classroom.

☐

That class of teachers in Missouri was a success. Their writing proved it. I had helped a number of these persons realize that if they could write more powerfully than they had suspected, then perhaps their students could also.

## Chapter 10

# *A Class That Wouldn't Talk*

□

... self-consciousness involves the individual's becoming an object to himself by taking the attitudes of other individuals toward himself within an organized setting of social relationships, and ... unless the individual had thus become an object to himself he would not be self-conscious or have a self at all.

George Herbert Mead, *Mind, Self & Society*
(Chicago: The University of Chicago Press,
1934), p. 225.

I looked forward to reading nine of Shakespeare's major plays again with college juniors and seniors. Year after year the combination of Shakespeare's range and depth and my students' fine response to it had made this class *buoyant* for me. I want that word here, for when classes are going well they possess that lightness that comes from our having fun pursuing an idea, seeing resemblances between the materials being studied and the lives of all of the persons meeting with each other to learn. That means much laughter and sometimes tightened lips as persons probe a matter together. And high seriousness of the kind that is often signaled by rolls of laughter which succeed one another like muttering thunder. I looked forward to another Shakespeare class.

This time I walked in the first day wondering if the lack of windows in the basement room would cloud the students' spirits. Forty of them I had to arrange in one large open square, everyone's chair against the wall. I started off as usual, and the second day found myself reading aloud to them some of the free writings I had asked them to do to loosen themselves up. Since I had talked about making this course freer and more lively than most college courses, I dittoed three of the free writings which touched on school.

*1*

*I have so much to do before it is the weekend again, and somewhere in the middle of it I have to go validate my I.D. I'm so fond of this university anyway. That's all I need. I'm surprised there's no fee for validating an I.D. I imagine nobody's thought of it yet. With all the money we pay them, you'd think they could heat the rooms. "The heat comes from the state hospital and there's nothing we can do to control it. Take a nail file and monkey with the vent." Look, lady—you monkey with the vent. God grant me the serenity to accept the things I cannot change. Becky is studying again. I really respect her for it but I sure wouldn't want to live her life. That sounds mean. I think I've gotten a whole lot meaner since I've been at Western. Somehow college brings out the worst in you. By Wednesday, I must make an achromatic and a chromatic tree, of all things, for art ed workshop. What's more important? That or the fact that I have to read the entire* Scarlet Letter *by that day and in my spare time read* Romeo and Juliet *and try to keep my parents and Becky and Bennie all happy and maintain Jane in their lives the way they want Jane to be. And then I cry. No less, I cry on the telephone. To my mother. That's really nifty. I was doing fine when I was talking to Dad and Bennie and Liz but Mom knows me too well. That was the night Bennie and I were engaged. Now that. I refuse to give up. All this isn't important and I won't let it interfere with my life. WMU is no longer first and foremost. It shouldn't ever have been. If I get all this stuff done, fine. If I don't, I'm sorry Western Michigan University, but you're not going to win this one. You have gotten me down too many times. I'm sick of teachers who feel they must be gross or crude to impress their students who in turn feel they must be gross and crude to impress the teacher—and I use that term very loosely. Teachers no longer teach. It's easier to hold an "Open Classroom." The kids may not learn anything but at least you're with the times. I am so sick of people being phony and forcing me to be phony.*

When I came on that paper in the batch it made me uneasy because I didn't want the students to think this was going to be an encounter group with the praise going to the student who confessed his sins most mawkishly. I was pleased to find that the writer of the following paper said he admired "open" classrooms. That meant I already had a discussion going on the dangers and virtues of open and closed classrooms.

2

*Tonight while watching the eleven o'clock news, the newscasters were showing films on "disturbances" in Baton Rouge, Louisiana. I have to admit I received a shock when upon my tube I witnessed through the miracle of tape (My, haven't we come far in the last twenty-five years?) a policeman bashing a protestor's, with the butt of his gun, head in. Much to my chagrin they even seemed to be doing some of news reporters in as well. This brings to mind a question (the way our school system is set up this is a rarity): Where have the Students for a Democratic Society been this past year? I have not heard or read anything concerning them recently. The grapevine has it that they are planning a coup d'état. Sure would like to see a coup in our educational system. It needs so much help that practically nothing short of doing it in could help it. Sure wish I had the opportunity to go to an open classroom when I was younger, then maybe my curiosity (the natural curiosity that young children all possess) might not have been thwarted as I believe it was. Just think, everything I knew by graduation of high school probably would have been learned by the 5th grade.*

(I noted the dangling participle in the first sentence of that entry, but I did not mention it to the student writer or the class. Tolstoy and I know we can freeze our students at the outset with comments like that.)

We had a good discussion of those two papers. I thought we all came away agreeing that one learns best when he is given both freedom and direction. There was a fine relaxed tone to that first discussion, brought on, I now think, by the writings, which manifested that rare quality of lightness I just mentioned.

In their journals and free writings many students in my classes tell their feelings about school. At first I feared they were trying to get in good with Teacher, because always on first day I make some disparaging remarks about the inanities of the education system which I upheld for so many years. But I no longer worry. The writers present their school experience too authentically to be merely echoing my opinions. They create that virtual life that convinces.

☐

In recent Shakespeare classes I had received several papers about students' experiences that illuminated the plays we were reading. For several years I had been getting an occasional paper of that kind, but I had waited until about two-thirds of the way along in the semester before suggesting the possibility to the whole class. I feared that too much attention to a student's own experience might lead him to read the plays superficially. In the first free writings in this Shakespeare class, I received this comment from a girl I'll call Patricia. It worried me. I don't care to play psychiatrist. I did not reproduce it for the class.

> So much has happened to me since the week before Thanksgiving. That's when I caught hepatitis and was isolated for five weeks. It was so painful being totally alone. I spent most of the time inside my head, building dreams, building my whole future life around the man I'd been living with, trying to stay sane. Then my whole world was crumbled just before I got back. He came and told me how he had gotten involved with one of the other girls in the house—my best friend, and I almost died. The two people I loved the most ripped me off and I couldn't bear it. I just couldn't understand how they could have done it when I called every day to ease some of my desperateness, when I sent my share of rent every week so as to ease the strain off my roommates. It was as if I was paying him to ball my roommate.
>
> But he came right back to me, yet I couldn't handle all the leftover bad feelings, the hate, the love turned around backwards. So I asked him to give me some time by myself so I could get some feelings together, and he bounced right back to my roommate. I never became so violent in all my existence. I had no idea of my physical strength. I lost touch with everything real for a while and became totally enveloped with my hate.
>
> He left the house so all could get their minds together. They kept meeting behind my back, and that twisted the knife even deeper. How much more can I survive? Finally, he and I spoke together and I took down my walls and showed him my heart and

*he did the same. The hate went away, but so did he. He's on the other side of the country, he won't be back for months. Since I've been back and all this has happened, and now I am alone, I spend my days trying to rid my mind of what's obsessing it. My night dreams are violent and disturbing, my day dreams are sad and remembering. My friend and I are tighter than ever before. She never thought I could forgive. I didn't either. But I am starting my living all over again. I am changed and tired. The strength must come from somewhere.*

Patricia's statement—I knew—had arisen out of the first discussion we had of *Romeo and Juliet*. A student had said the young lovers' urge toward suicide was unbelievable.

As usual, I had assigned this play as the first to be read. Ordinarily I take the nine plays I have chosen in chronological order, to help students see something of Shakespeare's development, and to work toward the high points of *Hamlet* and *King Lear*. But the discussion in class of *Romeo and Juliet* was halting. I decided to let the students hear a play; maybe that would unlock their tongues. So I played the whole record of John Gielgud's *Hamlet*, starring Richard Burton, who reads the part as I think Shakespeare would have wanted it read. That excited the class and they wrote fine notebook entries on the play.

*"Call me what instrument you will, though you can fret me, you cannot play upon me." (p. 111) This passage has got to be one of the best I've ever read. I get furious when people try to pick me apart—to discover the "real" me. I don't even know the real me—but I intend to spend my life finding out. Until I do, I sure don't want some punk like Guildenstern to come along and "sound me from my lowest note to the top of my compass." (111) Revelations of this sort are shared with a friend—a trusted friend. Rosencrantz and Guildenstern commit a horrible act as far as I can see it. They use friendship as a cover. These dear "friends" spy for the King to tear Hamlet down. The more I think about it, the madder I get. This is my "unpardonable sin."*

*I have often been accused of "keeping to myself." Is it any wonder? Things like the betrayal of a trust hurt. They hurt long and deep. Characters like Rosencrantz and Guildenstern are—unfortunately—not confined to a Shakespeare play. They're a dime a dozen, and their motives are endless.*

*Last Saturday I worked at the desk from 7 am to 10 am. At that time of the morning, the desk is a totally dead place. The dorm director came out of her apartment and realized that I was there alone. So she came in—as she said—"to keep me company." I thought that was decent of her, because most college students are non-existent at 7 am on Saturday morning and it can really get dull by yourself. My gratitude lasted about 3 minutes—or until the question, "What's the situation with drugs on your floor?" It totally ended with "If you hear of anything that will help me cement my case, let me know." Pumping session over. Result: I'll never trust that dumb woman again.*

*This probably sounds cynical or paranoid. It's just that I turn off to people with motives. There are a lot of people I trust to the extent that they probably know more about me than I do. But they're people who aren't going to use me or turn on me or hurt me. And that's something very special.*

Again, one of my students had precisely located the quality and intensity of a Shakepeare character's feeling—in this instance, Hamlet's cynicism and apparent paranoia.

Another student wrote:

*Ever since Thursday I've been trying to think of something to write about. Finally it came to me that I had a sort of Hamlet-ish experience in my own family. It was like Hamlet in that it involved a son's antipathy toward one of his parents but it wasn't quite as dramatic as Hamlet because nobody died or anything. When my dad was about 16 his dad all of a sudden left home and moved about 12 miles away. After a short period of time, after an uncontested divorce from his wife, he took another wife. My dad had to start helping out with the income because he had three younger sisters at home, plus his mom. No one would have anything to do with my grandpa. I think my dad thought he was just about the rottenest son of a bitch that walked on the earth. Finally, when he was about 21, he and my mother decided to get married. He wasn't even going to tell his dad about it or anything. Then just before the big day my mom said that he couldn't go through life hating his father. So I guess they went to him and told him about their plans and then, after dad had gone to him, the other relatives slowly began to drift back to see him. It took a while but everything supposedly worked out okay. It's funny but I still think my dad never really did forgive his father for what he did. I wonder if I would.*

At this time Patricia wrote the following entry in her notebook:

*I really see how Hamlet feels when it comes to his mother and uncle. When I was away from home for five weeks, the man who had been living with me for months started doin' a thing with my roommate, my best friend. It's like I didn't exist with them any more. I couldn't comprehend how, when they both loved me, they could hurt me so. I saw what fools they were, like Gertrude and Claudius, to succumb to their lower animal passions of desire, of selfishness. "What fools these mortals be." I felt like a god when I came back, as I think Hamlet did, above the fools, the epitome of self-control and conscienceness ('cause you just don't ball unsciencely).* [I think Patricia meant *conscious* here, but the play between the two words makes both meaningful in this context.] *In the past I had pushed some of her lovers away when they approached me, so what weakness kept her from doing the same?*

*Hamlet, being above them, was obsessed with the godly revenge of his father's death, obsessed with the painful conscienceness and insight of the weakness of the human animal, the selfish flesh. He felt like the controller of the situation, the insanity of really seeing "Where do you go when you don't want to know what you know?"*

I thought this a helpful statement. I read it to the class without identifying the author or giving out a copy of it. Many students come to *Hamlet* with the popular notion that the prince is just a moody fellow constitutionally unable to make up his mind, so they do not confront the facts of his pressured situation. But Patricia saw how the bizarre nature of Hamlet's condition skewed him. Nevertheless, as her second comment on her personal experience, it worried me: was she ever going to discuss the plays directly? When I encourage students to bring their experience up against the experience of a university course, I warn them they may lose all objectivity and distort the materials of the course to fit their presuppositions. She had not distorted the plays, but I began to fear that she would see nothing in them that she had not already experienced herself.

☐

Only two or three students in the class besides Patricia were willing to talk, even when I reproduced journal entries on the plays and offered them for discussion. I asked, "What's wrong? Why don't you talk?" The answer was appropriate—silence. After class a student said she thought the class was too large, maybe it needed to be broken into small groups for discussion. I arranged that on one day a week the class would be split into two sections, each one meeting with me for an hour. The class met twice a week, and at the other meeting we all came together as usual.

At the first small-group meeting the talk improved. During the second hour, when I met with the other half of the class, only about eight students showed up and Patricia, as usual, began the discussion. (I should correct myself to say that the small number of students present was partly due to the fact that about two-thirds of the class had found the first hour more convenient and a larger proportion always met at that time.) Patricia spoke for ten minutes, telling some more harrowing stories of her own recent experience. One other student spoke up, trying to break in, but Patricia listened only a minute and then got back on her track. What she said was fascinating and at points paralleled the experience in the play we were studying, but I noticed several of the others looked frustrated. One turned off and began looking at the wall. This was the moment—freed from the pressure of speaking to the large class—when I had hoped all the students would get into the habit of speaking up. When there were ten minutes left in the hour I interrupted Patricia and tried to turn the talk to a point one of the other students had made briefly. That night when I went home I determined I would have to tell Patricia of the dangers of talking too much in a class in which talk by everyone was essential.

At the next class meeting, Patricia handed me this note:

> *I was really disappointed in you the other day in class. At the beginning of the semester you gave the strong impression that we were to relate and involve ourselves as much as possible in the plays to make them meaningful. Now, when we are getting very involved and are relating very heavily, why do you cut us off? Why do you run away?*
>
> *I have paid seventy-two dollars for you to touch me, Macrorie, for you to teach me, but you do not allow us to touch back, to reach you. It's a two way street.*
>
> *I can understand why, if you cannot relate to our projections, or if what we speak of makes you question yourself.*
>
> *Please, don't be afraid to grow with us.*

I answered her with my own note:

> Last Thursday I determined I must talk to you about the danger of your making the discussion period a monologue about your own experiences. In my estimation you came right up to the edge of losing your audience. Some—maybe one or two—hung on with you. Others began to sigh and look away. I study these things, that's my job. I thought you were making some fine observations; once in a while you seemed to ramble, and seldom did you come back squarely to the Shakespeare play so those who had not been thinking of it through your experience could always know what you were speaking to in Shakespeare. At one point I remember cutting you off. No matter how perceptive you are and how profound your connections between your experience and the plays, if you dominate discussion after discussion, you will lose the ear of your fellow students. I want you to hang back at times, remember you're one in 12 or one in 40. That is as essential to the richness of their experience of the class as your giving them your richness. And I want you to come forth occasionally speaking fully and strongly as you can.

I prefer not to have this direct encounter arise—either my singling out a student or he me. A class is not a one-to-one experience. It is a bunch of people coming together, with individuals coming forth strongly with their opinions and feelings, but always to the group, not just to one other person, a student or teacher. I think life is hard in one-to-one. I think of my wife and I who manage most of the time to get along well together. If we did not each have our consuming and gratifying work—she her etching and jewelrymaking and writing, and I my teaching and writing—I doubt that we would make it together. For our work allows us both to get away from each other into something rich and challenging, and also it gives us an objective other thing than ourselves to talk about. So our encounters are not always, "Mr. Macrorie, you have failed me today. Or Patricia, I think you are collapsing in this course."

As I look at that note now, I think how hard it is for me to write anyone briefly, and I remember that in my college days, both undergraduate and graduate, professors always seemed to say too much when they were attacked or countered.

☐

Several weeks later I noticed that Mrs. Bremington, who wrote thoughtful journal entries, was not talking at all. I couldn't remember a word from her. Most of the time her face remained expressionless. Another student or I would make what I thought was a humorous point. I would look directly at her: impassive. So before the class started one day I asked her to come out in the hall where I pleaded with her to talk more, assuring her I thought she was one of the most intelligent persons in the class. In low and strained voice she said, "I think that a teacher who asks a reluctant talker to talk is apt to freeze him up forever." I could see that possibility, but my experience with many other students had proved otherwise. So back to class we went, Mrs. Bremington to sit cold and silent, I to become more anxious.

In past years I had always begun the class with a half-hour talk on Elizabethan language, assuring the students I wouldn't be testing them on vocabulary, pointing out both the foreignness and similarity between our American-English of the day and Elizabethan language. "Don't be surprised," I would say, "that Elizabethans used a slang and depended a lot on idiomatic expressions. We do too. When the Nurse says than the man who's got the chinks will get Juliet she's using a metaphorical word like our *bread* or *green stuff*."

On another day I customarily gave a little talk about sexual references in *Romeo and Juliet*. I had discovered that although my students are more sexually liberated and knowledgeable than my generation, they often miss the metaphorical allusions to sex in this highly sexual play. Because the students in this class had talked so maturely and easily about school on the first day, I decided to dispense with discussions like these from me. They would not be necessary. And the sooner I could get them thinking for themselves and bringing their knowledge and experience to bear upon the course, the more learning would take place.

☐

The discussion on *Hamlet* was first-rate. Most of the students had heard the recording of the whole play in class. I duplicated about sixteen of their papers and we discussed them, both in the large class and in the smaller groups. It was a fine discussion. They faced the shock of their differing opinions and probed more deeply into the play. As usual, some of the observations were new to me, a teacher who had "taught" *Hamlet* eleven times.

Since the university theater was presenting *King Lear* in February, I decided to urge students to see it and to make it the third play we read in class rather than, as usual, the eighth. I recognized the danger of departing from chronological order: a student moving from *Hamlet* and *King Lear*, flowers of Shakespeare's later years, might find the earlier *Richard II* one-dimensional. All but a handful of the students attended the showing of *King Lear*, which was done with unusual skill. The ensuing papers and discussions were sharp and enthusiastic.

From then on the class went downhill. The papers remained lively and perceptive, but discussion often came to a standstill. Many students grew sour as they listened to their papers read in class. I tried to keep up my confidence. I began each class with what I thought was a positive note in my voice and invited responses to the plays as if I were sure they would be forthcoming. They weren't. In some of the papers students began to complain that *Richard II* and *Henry IV, Part I* were dull. I wished Shakespeare had been there to hear them. Ordinarily such frankness is the beginning of debates that bring out the strengths and weaknesses of a play. Many students didn't turn in their papers on time; when I received them I found a number that would have made the complainers see more depth in the plays, but by then it was too late to reproduce them and use them in discussion. We were moving ahead with another play. Silences grew. I waited and waited for students to say what they thought about Falstaff, and they had few words—the first time in my experience as a teacher of Shakespeare.

The papers and journal entries continued at a high level, but when I read them to the class, they seldom elicited a spirited discussion. I would say, "What do you think of that? How did that paper strike you?" Nothing. I would ask again. We would all squirm, except Mrs. Bremington, whose jaw clenched more tightly and Patricia—who sat sulking in her chair—if she was present. She began cutting class frequently. Finally a student would speak up. I would comment more than I wanted to. The room became a torture chamber. In the course that had always been so easy, relaxed, and inquiring, I was now forcing myself not to scream, "Goddamnit, people, say something!"

Four weeks before the end of the semester, I came upon this paper.

> *Twice a week I tread into the first floor of Brown Hall to discuss the works of my good friend Will Shakespeare. Strangely, I find that regardless of what mood I am in when I enter the classroom. I will turn sour with despair within ten minutes. One would think I was attending Mortuary Science 101.*
>
> > *Oft I have to pinch my arse*
> > *Lest I think myself amongst a heap o' corses.*
> > *Most abject souls make class a farce*
> > *And I think more discourse could be had with horses.*
>
> *If we chose to have a documentary made on one class period we would call it* Day of the Living Dead *or* Trapped in the Cavern of Zombies. *I think if some of the people in class forced themselves to laugh, smile, or otherwise control their features, their faces would break.*
>
> *Whatever happened to the good old days when students were human beings with feelings and emotions? It's frightening to see how many of us have become automatons, surpassed in coldness only by Mr. Spock on* Star Trek. *Most of us live by the code: "Memorize the facts and vomit them back to the teacher and that's all there is to it."*
>
> *There is such a lack of interaction in this class that if I were the instructor teaching this class of noble stone faces I would be tempted to walk out of the class and do something more constructive, like talking to chimpanzees in the zoo. At least they do something. I don't think I would have the patience to see forty people numbly listen to the most hilarious lines of Falstaff in* Henry IV, Part One, *as if it was a funeral eulogy, without going apeshit.*
>
> *And when the papers are passed out, everybody scurries through to see if they are among the anointed ones to be revered by the masses, thinking:*
>
> > *I shall see if I shall be among the chosen few*
> > *Whose scriptures doth merit a classwide review.*
> > *But if my paper is not deemed so well*
> > *Then this bastardly class can disperse to hell.*
>
> *So it comes to pass that the chosen few try to hold together a discussion among themselves while the thirty neglected souls gaze*

daggers at the lucky ones, determined not to contribute their two cents worth come hell or high water.

(This is where I tie this paper into the Shakespearean theme.) In Richard II, I came across a very human trait which I think lies at the heart of the problems we have been having in this class.

Richard is a flatterer of high degree, yet he has great disdain toward the flatterers who accost him. Could it be that Richard thinks:

> 'Sblood! His flowery affections doth swoon the soul.
> But so obvious is the lack of heart in his message
> That the words come to me as rain upon the roof;
> They roll off me without dampening me within.
> I wonder, therefore, might my own flattery
> Be so samely false in the eyes of all by mine?
> Truly, he smells most readily on others
> That rottened stench which he himself gives off,
> Wondering all the while if his own stench
> Gives off so foul an odour.

In this sense I can see how I am seeing how unsociable everyone else is in the light of how aloof I am during class. No doubt the rest of the class is at the same standstill, glowering at the person next to them, condemning them for not being more friendly, when they themselves sit in their chairs like mannequins, lost to the world around them in their own individual tragedies.

It is sad enough to run across characterless characters in Richard II, but the despair I feel comes from constantly running into living human beings on this campus who are afraid to show their personality and henceforth adopt a stiff, robot-like behavior wherever they go.

Bob Gillet had risked turning this statement in as a formal paper, one of the four that would determine his grade for the course. His gesture made me think once more of the power of the grading system. Bob was an extraordinarily confident young man; few students would take such a risk. I thought his paper might well be the act that would bring this class together again in conversation that would illuminate Shakespeare's plays. I read his paper to the class, expecting it to release the pent-up feeling. A few smiles, a few scowls, two short comments from students, and then the usual silence, looking down or around, as if expecting someone else would take the responsibility of talking.

I waited for more comment. None. Then I said I felt the students in this class were unusually reluctant to speak but that I had to accept most of the blame if a class didn't go well. I could shape the class any way I wished, and it was my job to make it one that nurtured good talk as well as good writing. I asked if anyone could guess why this Shakespeare class was the first in twelve I had taught which wouldn't talk.

Again a long silence, and we could only laugh. I don't believe the students knew any better than I what made them taciturn. I suggested that perhaps I shouldn't have put *Hamlet* and *Lear* so early in the class, that maybe I should have talked more myself so they didn't feel so much of the success of the class depended on them. One student said the papers were mostly trivial and not worth discussing. Several others said they had learned a lot from the papers. No one explanation received enough support to convince many persons.

I went back to Bob's paper, saying I thought it was an accurate description. After the praise, I theatrically attacked its weaknesses: Bob had mistakenly used the Elizabethan *doth* as a plural verb, and he had written two clichés in a row. Some of the students caught my ironical humor: this was the first time in class I had pointed out mistakes "like an English teacher should."

From that day on the attendance dropped drastically. About twenty of the forty turned up faithfully every day and spoke a little more freely, but the chill dampness of failure had settled in over that room.

Another student had responded in her journal to my comments that I was mainly responsible for the deadness of the class.

*Last Thursday I knew I wanted to write you and tell you how much good this class is doing me. I thought that Mr. Macrorie would like to hear how I felt and it would probably do him some good, too. Today I knew I had to write. What's this business about not succeeding with your Shakespeare class? Not going well and getting behind?*

*On a typical day after class I leave feeling and thinking of Shakespeare at a rate of 100 M.P.H. For the rest of the day the thinking will hang over me, controlling my thinking. Shakespeare, Shakespeare, Shakespeare. He becomes an instrument probing my different brain centers. Each time a different center is touched I see a new image, side, idea exposed. Wow. To seriously ponder, to think like this, makes me feel like I'm something of worth. Worth something to this class, but mostly worth myself. I feel tall, I have something to share. It even makes me feel better that this is so even for one person. No one can say what you said today. I want to go on. More Shakespeare! More Shakespeare! Maybe I'm different. I must have a Shakespeare seed in me, but not everyone does and that's the way it is. So, Mr. Macrorie, I feel like you're wrong. I know this is your job and you do your job and next time you start thinking it's going poorly you should just say "Fuck it," because you're not ever going to reach all and probably not even half. I'm very lucky if I'm the only one to be reached.*

The girl who wrote that had been doing beautifully, contributing ideas and enthusiasm that should have turned on a good share of the class. But I told the student I would have none of that argument. If a class of forty was to be justified by the good experience of one student, it was a misuse of everyone else's time and money.

I felt like saying it was all over, go home and we'll meet on the last day to get grades. But I didn't. Too much pride. I restored my practice of occasionally talking on a subject that interested me. For example, I furnished a number of unidentified lines from plays by Shakespeare's contemporaries and suggested that his command of language was seldom greater than Christopher Marlowe's or Beaumont's or Fletcher's, or Webster's at their best, but that overall he worked with greater range and complexity. I could tell the faithful were interested. Now I am sure they found my speaking for half an hour or an hour refreshing after all those hours in which they had felt the responsibility for carrying the talk in that class. I had forgotten one of my principles of teaching: to alternate kinds of activities, introduce opposites.

As is my habit in the Shakespeare class near the end of the course, I began to reveal some of my personal likes and dislikes, and the students began to reveal theirs. We had two fine discussions on the inadequacies of *The Merchant of Venice* and *The Tempest*. Rich and lively as they are, we found them wanting as unified works and we suspected Shakespeare was not sure what he was trying to do in them. I began these sessions with my own criticisms and spoke at length, but the students were not afraid to add theirs. Those few who attended the last few weeks regularly were captivated by Shakespeare and willing to suffer awkward silences to be near him. The last three weeks were not entirely unproductive.

All through that course the students had written thoughtful papers and journal entries. There was never a batch of papers that did not contain provocative comments. For example:

#### 1

*I do not like to be treated as an idiot, yet I get this feeling from Shakespeare. It seems that immediately after any action in the play he sets up some flunky to give a synopsis of what has just happened. At the end he engages in a game of ring around the cast to tell the entire play in two pages, as if I were too stupid to know what was going on. This grossly undermines the play, giving us the impression that either Shakespeare was unconfident of his ability to playwrite or else his audience's ability to understand him. Both cases are self-defeating.*

#### 2

*I think that thing at the end about Macduff being "not of woman born" was pretty sloppy. Either Shakespeare should have found a different way of getting a man "not of woman born" or else* dropped the whole thing. I was born by caesarian and I am considered to be of woman born. I don't feel like a supernatural being. I know that Shakespeare dug tricking, turning of phrases, and double meanings but I think he is stretching a point past believability here.

### 3

I've got a question. Did witches have the same meaning to people in Macbeth's time as they do now? I couldn't understand why he listened to them. Man, if I saw three witches I wouldn't stick around to ask questions, let alone believe what they said.

Few students were satisfied to settle back into the rut of giving us the safe and obvious. They had got the message at the outset: when they wrote they were to put down what surprised them and might surprise the rest of us. Many of their papers carried the sound of authority that comes from commanding materials and speaking honestly. For example:

### 4

Prince Hal in Henry IV was the most unbelievable character I have ever read. We see Hal at the beginning of the play as the equivalent of a hippie—he has turned his back on his family, and on the obligations and responsibilities as Prince of Wales, and spends his time fraternizing with characters of such ill repute as Falstaff, drinking cheap wine and stealing. Hal has evidently "dropped out" of the establishment.

He is a very likeable character at this point. I found myself identifying with him, and wishing I were in the same position. All Hal had to do was sit back, drink, and exchange witty thrusts with Falstaff. He had time to play long, involved practical jokes, and he seemed to have an endless supply of money. They even joked about the King, Hal's father, and about his attitude toward his son when they performed the parody: "Why being son to me [Falstaff], art thou so pointed at?" They mock the King and in mocking him end up ignoring him completely while they turn their attention to the relative merit of Falstaff's dubious virtue.

The King doesn't think Hal is so funny, though. In fact, he wishes that by some mistake Hal and Hotspur had gotten switched at birth and "it could be proved that some night-tripping fairy" had exchanged one son for the other. So, for the first two and one-half acts, Hal is seen as a rebel against the rigors of responsibility, who simply doesn't give a damn about his father, or England, or comporting himself in princely fashion.

That seemed to me to be an admirable attitude, and up until Hal has the confrontation with his father, I thought he was the most likeable character I've read in Shakespeare. However in Act III, Hal does a complete about-face. Whereas before, he had neither the time nor the inclination to get involved in political intrigue, now after listening to two paragraphs from his father he is ready to recant, put down the bottle and pick up a sword and defend King and country to the death. After the King tells Hal how he has retained his aura of glamour in the kingdom by making himself scarce, and how Hal will never be popular as a king because the people are too familiar with him, Hal simply says, "I shall hereafter, my thrice-gracious lord,/Be more myself." After hearing only one paragraph worth of lecture from the King, Hal comes back into the fold, forgets Falstaff and Eastcheap and his own mockery of his father.

Things get worse. After listening to the King praise Hotspur as "Mars in swathling, this infant warrior," Hal swears to "wear a garment all of blood, and stain my favors in a bloody mask, which, washed away, shall scour all my shame." Now Hal, who throughout the play never engaged in combat more rigorous than robbing from thieves as a joke, wants to "Redeem all this on Percy's head . . . and be bold to tell you that I am your son." For someone who previously showed utter disdain for anything having to do with royalty, he certainly is eager to please his father by getting rid of Hotspur.

Out on the battleground, Hal's dreams all come true, as he runs Hotspur through, but not before Hotspur lavishes praise on him as being "so sweet a hope, so much misconstrued in his wantonness," regains his favor in the eyes of the King ("Thou hast redeemed thy lost opinion"), and even finds out his brother John is not such a bad kid after all. It seems to all have come out in the wash. Hal is even ready to agree in a burst of generosity that it was Falstaff who killed Hotspur. This is a complete contradiction of his earlier reaction to Falstaff's lies—Hal never let Falstaff get away with a lie in the Eastcheap days, but now he is willing to admit that Falstaff was the killer just so everybody is happy.

I don't think Hal's capitulation to his father was in itself unbelievable, but the way he was so eager to give in without argument was too contrived. He was anti-princedom one day and out defending the crown the next, and he never even gave any thought to why or how he changed his mind and his life-style so quickly.

☐

When the course came to an end and I was making out grades, I experienced a return of feelings I hadn't had so strongly since 1963, the year before my students had first broken through. I wanted to get back at some of these people for refusing to talk and for cutting class so much. I tried to fight down the feeling. I knew my actions more than anything else had hurt that class. I had put too much of the responsibility for talk on the students. I had begun the class with the strongest plays instead of sticking to a developing order. But still those reasons did not sufficiently explain the students' reluctance to speak. These young people had been trained for years to be sheep, to listen to Teacher, to give him back what they thought he wanted to hear. But so had others in my Shakespeare classes, and they had talked beautifully. I let myself get extra angry at a few students who had not turned in papers or had cut so many classes that their late papers did not show the sophistication and depth that comes from hearing what other students have written and said.

I arranged that the last paper of four would be due March 30, twenty days before the end of the semester, so my students wouldn't be overloaded with papers when they were studying for exams in other courses. Then at a later date I would ask them to hand in all their papers at once for a grade. Some time after that first due date a young man came up to me and said, "Here's my papers." I was infuriated and said coldly, "The last of four papers was due two weeks ago and now you're handing these to me?" He looked bewildered. I took them from him and noticed they all carried comments in my handwriting. He explained that he had previously turned all of them in on time and simply had forgotten to bring the batch to me for the grade. He walked away shaking his head. I felt someone else had been talking for me. I had been vindictive. My action demeaned me as well as him.

I am not saying that a teacher should never be harsh. Frequently when I have been hard on a student he has come back to another of my classes, and sometimes he has become a friend; but only when I have acted on justifiable grounds. For years the system taught me to hate students: lecture to them, test them, and show anger when they become bored or frustrated. In this Shakespeare class I tried—as I have learned to do in recent years—to let the students' work teach them. I withheld grades on papers until the end of the semester so they would study each other's papers and judge what they thought was valuable to the others. Occasionally when a student had been missing class or continuing a weakness in paper after paper, I wrote him a note; but my experience tells me that generally carping and picking at students does no more good than my telling my stepdaughters to return the 7-Up bottle to its carton after finishing it. Here are two such notes to students in that class, the first one to Patricia.

Your first paper, like Bob Gillet's about *Hamlet*, helped the class. I read it though it didn't make a case directly from the play. It took for granted that the other students knew the play well enough to know why you were making your general assertions, just as Bob's paper did. That worked well with *Hamlet*, which the class knew better than the other plays. In your other papers you took a bigger risk. I am sure you convinced some who were already leaning your way, but as I said several times in remarks on your papers, you needed to begin making a case with lines and quotes and citations of specific incidents or acts from the plays—if you were to be as convincing as in the *Hamlet* paper. For example, the remark that Portia was "horny." That would come as an unbelievable statement to a number of students in class who saw her as heroic. You needed there to show what lines, acts, speeches you based that assumption on. Your papers were among the most refreshing to read in the class. A number of other students wrote still more convincing papers.

Another "of course" parents' nag. I knew that Patricia wasn't going to change her ways because of it. It would take her peers as well as me to make her see any weakness in her performance. She was feeling exposed that semester. When she was criticized, she did not reflect on what was said, she struck back. I'm not sure whether the following note to another student had any positive effect. It was purposely strong and personal.

Demonstrate the "extreme" wise man Henry IV. Make your case. You need to do that on point after point in your paper. You should know if you had attended class frequently that these fellow-students of yours are not going to be convinced by a few general assertions. This is a frighteningly weak paper from a person with a mind like yours. If you came to class and contributed, you would raise the tone and you would also learn that there are other intelligent persons present. I was shocked by your late appearance in the class, your announcement, cool, that you had arrived, with no explanations. And then your growing absences. I don't give college credit to persons who don't take my courses. Not that they're all great, but I believe one who goes to college should go to college. Many intelligent persons choose other alternatives.

I hope I was right in writing that note. So easy to use the position to be sadistic. The hardest students to deal with are those who don't appear in class enough to get a sense of what the other students and I are doing.

□

One of the students—I'll call him Slibbard—appeared two or three times and then I never saw him. I tried to phone him but never succeeded. Halfway through the course I asked the others if they knew what had happened to him—"Is he sick, dropped out?" Some who knew him laughed, "No, he's around." After the course was over, the last class held, and the grades given out, I received a letter.

> *Dear Dr. Macrorie:*
> *I have tried to get in touch with you, but I didn't try hard enough I guess. I also didn't try soon enough.*
> *Enclosed is one of the four papers for your Shakespeare class.*
> *If it is at all possible could I receive an incomplete in your class that I could make up by doing the other papers over Spring term?*
> *I would like to meet with you to explain why I stopped coming to class and to talk about my papers and grade.*
> *I will be here for Spring and then graduating, so I know I would make it up right away.*
> *Thank you for your consideration and I will contact you soon as Spring Term begins.*
>
> *Sincerely,*
> */s/John J. Slibbard, Jr.*

I wanted to thank young Slibbard. He gave me a chance to release some of my anger about my miserable failure with that class. The paper he had turned in is a classic of "research" done by high-school and college students. No teacher wants to receive it but thousands teach their classes so they do. I haven't seen one like it since 1964. I reproduce it here so the reader can compare it with the papers I have presented by students taught another way:
[On a cover sheet]:

## THEATRE IN SHAKESPEARE'S DAY

*Shakespeare*
*John J. Slibbard, Jr.*

> *Prior to Shakespeare's birth in 1563 and during his youth theatre was performed by amateur groups and was trouped from place to place. They performed at fairs, festivals, courts and inyards. [sic] The trade guilds also did plays at the times of religious pageants.*
> *The plays were primarily religious and moral dramas that were used to teach the people.*
> *To get around they traveled in wagons and carried portable stages that were set up where they would play. At the back of these stages curtains were hung for the purpose of concealing the actors and for use in exits and entrances, but there was no other scenery used. For the most part the audiences were common crowds consisting of drunks, beggars and ruffians.*

*The acting companies were generally sponsored by nobles and in 1576 James Burbage, who was a member of the Earl of Leicester's company built the first permanent theatre outside of London. It consisted of a wooden frame enclosing an open courtyard. At one end of the courtyard was the stage, which was still portable. The theatre contained three balconies, had no seats and did not have a roof. Later, when the stage became permanent, the theatre received a roof, but the main courtyard was still under the open sky.*

Such exquisite prose! Straight—I'll bet—from a badly written book in the library. To receive a roof, or to remain under the open sky—what a fine dilemma.

*The stage was still clear of scenery, although at the back of it there were two doors. These led to a retiring room for the actors, and it was similar to the greenrooms in our modern theatres. There the actors could rest and change costumes, if needed. Also there were windows in the balcony over the stage. These were used for scenes, musicians and at times for the audience. A trap door in the stage floor represented hell and the roof over the stage was painted to look like the sky.*

*On the day of the performance colored curtains were hung around the bottom of the stage. Black was for tragedies, comedies, histories and pastorals were red, white and green.*

*Burbage's theatre was torn down in 1598 and rebuilt in 1599 as the Globe. It was built the same as the other theatre, but with benches placed in the balconies. The main yard where the "groundlings" sat still had no benches.*

*The Globe was where Shakespeare wrote, worked and acted. He was also part owner of the theatre. One interesting fact is that James Burbage's son Richard was a famous actor and he is the one that first performed "Hamlet," "Lear" and "Othello."*

Slibbard, I tend not to believe a word you're saying. How do you know all these things? Haven't you got the wrong author for *Othello*? Wasn't that written by Beaumont and Fletcher?

*On the days of performances a flag was raised at the theatre to show the people that there was to be a performance that afternoon. The audience would come early in the afternoon and it consisted mainly of men. Women who went were not respectable. This held true as far as the acting was concerned also.*

Slibbard, are you insinuating something about Queen Elizabeth?

Most of them entered through a main gate and paid the price of one penny. For more money they could get into the balconies. A few people paid more and were allowed to enter from the back way and were allowed to sit on the stage. This was very distracting to both the audience and the actors because these people would sit there and show off and interrupt the performance.

Above the stage was a hut that contained machinery. In it also were placed cannons that were used during battle scenes and for festivities. During a performance of "Henry VIII" the cannons were being used and a piece of hot wadding flew out onto the roof and set it on fire. This was in 1613 and the entire building was destroyed, although there was no loss of life. The Globe was then rebuilt but it was torn down in 1644 to make room for tenements.

Hodges, C. Walter; Shakespeare's Theatre
    Oxford Univ. Press, 1964
Marek, Hannelore; History of the Theatre
    Odyssey Press, N.Y., N.Y.: 1964
Roberts, Vera Mowry; On Stage
    Harper and Row, N.Y., N.Y.; 1962

Slibbard, you wonderful guy—a bibliography too! You did the job the system calls for. You weren't around enough to know that your fellow students heard different voices.

I sat down and wrote him a controlled, scathing letter and I felt better. But there was no point to that. He was playing the game according to the rules. My sense of gaining revenge upon the class was misplaced. Slibbard was one matter, my failure to get that class talking powerfully was another. He and I had both done badly in English 252.

# Epilogue

☐

Here it is a year later. In my most recent Shakespeare class the students wrote such full and penetrating journal responses to the plays that I felt obliged to extract the best writing and shape it into an anthology article for a magazine. But they, too, seldom talked to each other and to me in the circle. I asked why and they replied with rationalizations that made no sense to me. "I don't talk because I know no one else will talk either." "I don't want to say anything about another person's journal entries because it's not cool to comment on other students' work." When I traveled around the country to talk to other teachers in colleges and high schools, I heard them say their students were also clamming up.

I am sure that other pressures besides these have shut their mouths. The Vietnam war, which students just before them protested, lasted too long. When it was over, the youth of the country were given no credit for early seeing its evil. No praise, no thanks, for being right and practical about such a profound matter. As I write, the job market for college-trained youth is shrinking, and those training to become professionals see few jobs available. In the last national election a number of college students attempted to reform political organization and failed, only to find the Watergate scandal emerge in the wake of their efforts. In the middle of a time marked by political corruption and general decadence, these young people have been hounded for smoking marijuana by elders who continue to get high on alcohol at their own drug parties. Like others in the society, these college students have decided—often without knowing they have made a decision—to play it safe, to keep quiet in the classroom for fear of saying something wrong in that environment saturated with the notion that there is always a right or wrong answer, always a grade to be wangled that will entitle them to get a job which brings material comforts if not a good life.

☐

I think my analysis of why students aren't talking now is valid. We are all individuals with unique powers but also members of society. When I was in college in 1936-40, most of my fellows were contained and cautious in their speech in public places, including the classroom. A small percent were activists who supported civil rights in the United States and the Spanish Loyalist cause against dictator Franco, but they were a smaller group than the activists of the late sixties. The majority of students of that time cared little about others' rights: they were out dancing and drinking with their acquaintances. We all live as individuals and as social beings, possessing amazing powers born of our unique experiences—though few of us exercise them vigorously. All of us bend under the pressure of the lifestyle of our peers.

From 1964 on, I found myself able to draw out the powers of many of my students and enable them to perform works that counted for them and other persons. Only a few teachers in the country were doing this. Most of the young activists' achievements had taken place outside the classroom, in spite of their formal education. These young people tried to change the balance of power between administration and students, and failed. They tried to change the regulations and lifestyle of dormitories and succeeded. A few teachers around the country created new conditions in the classroom that allowed students to do things there that were thoughtful, positive, useful.

My students now are not talking but I do not despair. There will always be new challenges for a teacher. Nine years ago students were not writing truths that counted for them in my classroom. Today they are. I know their powers. If they become reluctant to use some of them, it is my job to find ways of releasing them again. I must never fall back into the teachers' trap of saying students are hopeless. Once I say that, I have said that I am hopeless, that I do not deserve to be paid for my work, which is essentially to open up and strengthen people who possess strengths. At the moment my challenge is to find ways of getting students to talk again. I will do that. They and I will find how to create new climates in which we will all grow.

☐

When I think of how to face students who look down when they face each other and me in the classroom, I am comforted by what they have taught me in the last nine years. They have shown me how their experiences can speak to mine and to the authoritative experience of the course. I know now how shaky is an enterprise founded entirely on intellectual supports. Yesterday I looked up the word *emotion* in the *Oxford English Dictionary*. It derives from Latin and means literally "motion out of"—*motion* plus *e* (short for *ex*). The dictionary cited a statement from a philosophical journal published in 1708: "Thunder

... caused so great an Emotion in the Air. ...." Emotion was then a physical movement, and I think it is now. A fine word to describe what proceeds from our experience—the developing perception that is organically a part of that experience. Thus emotion stands below intellect—or abstraction and generalization—and is more substantial because it is fuller, connected to its origins by blood vessels and muscles, rather than by symbols removed from the physical which we all are.

Again and again I have seen students go to their experience, pull it out of the past, and make it touch their present activity and ideas, knowledge, and experience of the experts. I know that such an act can more easily become for young persons than for old persons as satisfying and habitual as eating and drinking.

I know that when one is moving in this way he can avoid the traps of purely intellectual motion. In the company of others he can learn to cherish mistakes, to commit himself in a way possible only to those not afraid of error, who have in their minds tests for themselves that are always performances, products, achievements—not an examination in which nothing more occurs than the retrieval of information someone else has delivered to them. And that these emotional people look for grades on their performance not in letters or numbers on a piece of paper but in the response of other human beings to their work, and—most significant of all—in the use to which the responders put this work.

The freedom to commit oneself, to create, is habitual in a person who has made himself vulnerable, open to his experience and that of others, in whatever form he may encounter it. The word *vulnerable* derives from *vuln*, Latin for *wound*. To become powerfully vulnerable is to expose oneself to possible wounds. One cannot create valuable things without risk. If he brings to the moment the best of his past experience, he comes on strong; and if he suffers then a wound, it will not disable him, because he is at his best, moving out of his full experience, healthy and strong. He is emotional as well as intellectual. He is growing out of himself and others.